Acknowledgements

WHERE does one begin in thanking the plethora of musical and personal influences, relationships, businesses and people involved in aiding a writer in the daunting task of assembling a manuscript such as this? Of all the "thank you's" possible, the first and foremost urgent place to begin is with my wonderful and amazing wife, Stefanie. Thank you, my love, for enduring my hours upon hours of time away from the family, not only for this manuscript, but for all things that required your loving patience and endurance, and for those things I will surely ask you to endure in the future. Additionally, my kids' support has been certainly not without due acclaim. The encouragement of a child is worth an hundred ovations.

My burden for moving forward with this book is self-inflicted. But without my students' drive, and without their parents' questions, I'd have had nowhere to begin, and no one with which *to* begin. Thank you, all of you, for being both catalyst, and fodder, for this material.

Of the influences that have moved me forward, advised me, inspired me or mentored me, there are a few who stand out immediately in my mind. As a graduate of the Atlanta Institute of Music, I found great friendships in the leadership and guidance of Tom Knight, Nite Driscoll, Bill Hart, Vitali Tkachenka, Randy Hoexter, Carl Culpepper, Chris Fragale, Creig Harber, Eric Sanders and Steve Riech.

I would also like to thank Chris Bowman of the Instrumental Music Academy in Roswell, GA (and former member of the Classics IV) for his friendship, and guidance.

I would also like to thank the countless musicians, industry professionals and artists for asking me to performing with them or just for tolerating me personally.

As to business, I cannot thank Matt Higginbotham enough for his solid craftsmanship, attention to detail and overall commitment to creating the best sounding and best quality drums I have ever played. I'm proud to be aboard Bootleg Drums as an endorser. As well, Soultone Cymbals has been absolutely stupendous in its personal attention to their artists as well as their cymbals. I have only outstanding things to say about them, their company and their product. Thank you for working with me.

All writing, editing, formatting, audio, video, performing, mixing, mastering, photography, cover design, layout, written music material, graphics and the website was/were done by … me.

THE ULTIMATE DRUM KIT LEARNING METHOD

A Teacher and Student Progressive Development Curriculum

BEGINNER THRU INTERMEDIATE

THE ULTIMATE DRUM KIT LEARNING METHOD

A Teacher and Student Progressive Development Curriculum

BEGINNER THRU INTERMEDIATE

http://udklm.com

TYRONE A. STEELE

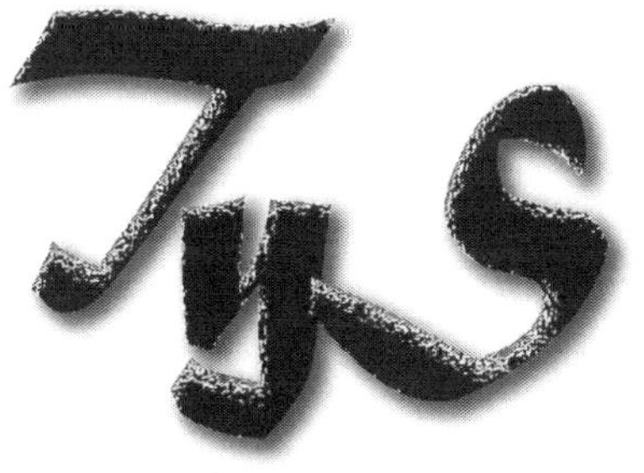

ISBN: 978-1507827123
ISBN-13: 1507827121

TABLE OF CONTENTS

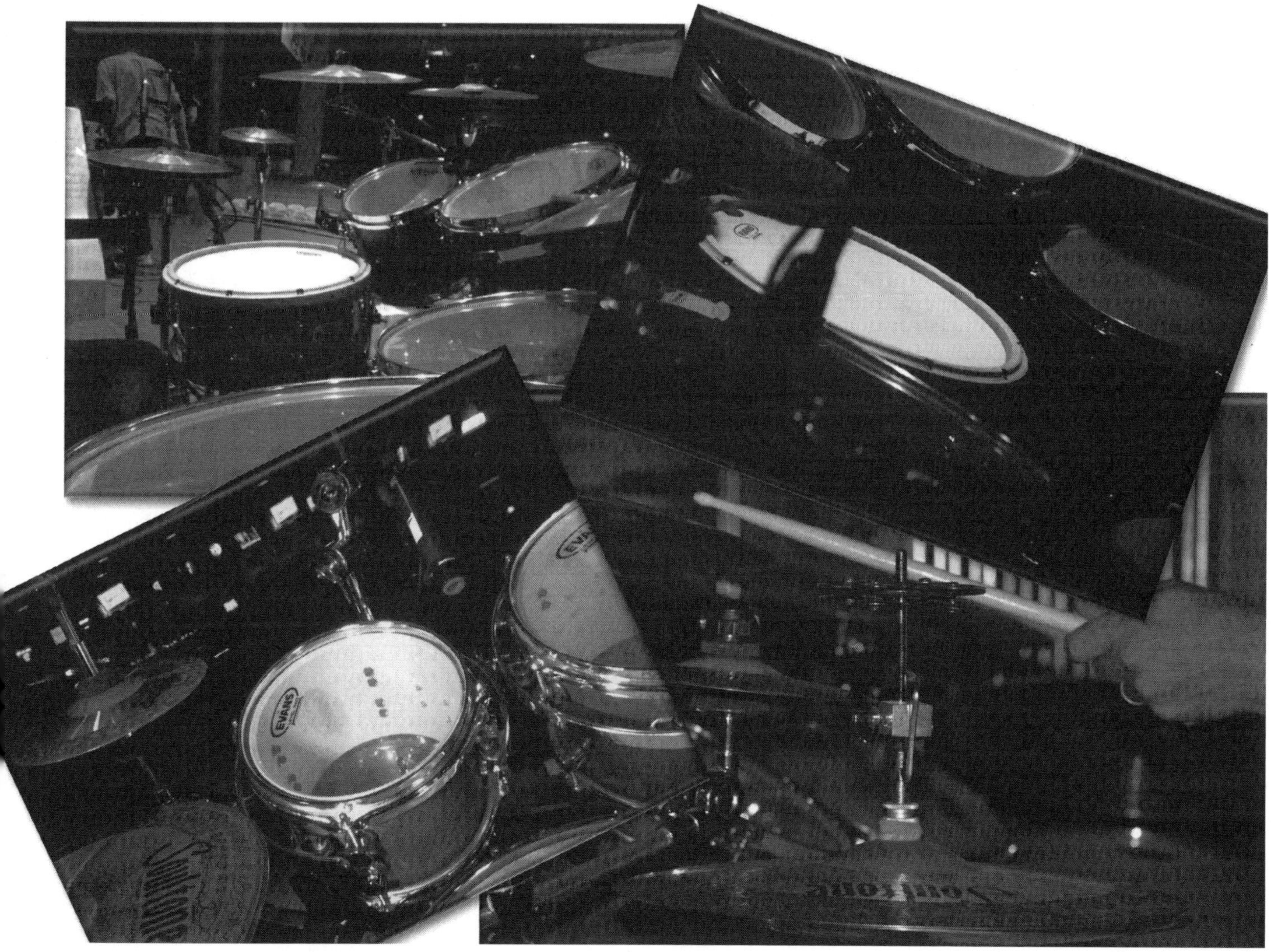

Setting the stage – Anderson Music Hall, Hiawassee, GA

Section I:
Introduction Material

A) Design, Purpose and Intent

Welcome! I'm glad you decided to join the ranks of either instructor or student for this marvelous instrument, the drumkit. I consider the drumkit to be the most original and beautiful instrument on the planet, or in all of human history. As an instructor or as a student (both of which I am), I hope that up to now things have gone well for you. If so, this book can certainly make life easier for learning and teaching the instrument; if not, this book was designed to help get you there.

Some years into teaching students of every age and level, from age six thru seventy-one, I had an idea. It was a career-altering idea. After tossing about with around eighty+ pages of material that I had amassed from years of teaching, after making copy after copy after copy for my students and for my own binder that I kept in a rigid order; after emailing PDF files to students and their parents; after counseling parents on invigorating their child, and on what gear to get them; after realizing that most students had entirely different versions of the same material and trying to juggle it unsuccessfully ... I finally decided to codex it all into one manuscript.

But that wasn't enough. That was just survival, more of a defensive maneuver, actually to keep my sanity and provide just *one* piece of material (no more extra books for students to buy), in one place, no copies to make or redistribute. No, that wasn't enough. Because actual teaching comes not from issuing piles upon piles of sheet music: it comes from the heart of the instructor. Additionally, it occurred to me that perhaps I could diminish the long-suffering of other instructors who are just getting started, plus provide a full step-through manual for the students as well.

In sections I thru III you will find introductory and reference materials for use at any time. Come back to those sections when you need a refresher in that information. In section IV of this book is the actual teaching material, the curriculum. Unlike other books, you will simply go from the first page of the curriculum to the last. You will find assignments in each segment. Each student should learn at his or her own pace, but do not 'leap' ahead of any assignment. I say with emphasis, *be sure you know each assignment well* before you move on to the next.

Belt Levels

And since I am a fan of mixed martial arts, and because there are so many similarities in training for both martial arts and the art of drumming, in my mind drumming is in belt-rank order, or levels. As a "**no belt**" you are just beginning: you know nothing, or very little, and what you do know will likely need correcting or reversing. As a "**white belt**" your knowledge has just begun: your understanding is blank like the white pages of an unwritten book. As a "**yellow belt**" your knowledge is like the rising sun: you have just started to see around the corner. "**Orange belt**" is explains that your drumming skills have become stronger like molten iron that is just beginning to set. As a "**green belt**" your skills and knowledge are becoming grounded like the roots of a plant.

And we stop there in this curriculum. In future curriculums you will see blue and red belts. Black is reserved for those who are approaching "master" levels. Not quite there, but only masters may teach them.

How This Book Differs From Others

The largest troubles I find with most drumkit books is that they are not oriented around actual *teaching*, not having defined an A thru Z method. Most of the successful (and timeless) books on drumming have mostly one thing in common: they are filled with virtually nothing but sheet music and take the student's skill level from A to Z. But even those timeless books to not address the *instructor*. That is the main difference. **This book is for both and meant to be used by instructor and student** for teaching and learning, respectively.

From beginning to end, this book reaches into the heart of teaching and learning. Remembering that my original intent was to address instructors, parents as well as students all in one codified manual, the additional impetus was to bring this method to other instructors for them and *their* students. This is a manual that instructors can use as well as their students. Everyone benefits – parents, students and instructors.

The advantage of this curriculum is the detailed instruction for each score (sheet of drum music), plus the meticulous arrangement of the material. Each score was designed with a purpose, with the intent to bring the student to the next level. For instance, the first section is simply reference materials: Rudiments, how to read drum music, *et cetera*. You will be referring to those materials often, and the student will need to go back to them again and again. The next section is where the student will begin: "*All 8th and 16th note Rhythms*." Section One is designed to create coordination, and is an introduction to rhythm. Triplets, swing and shuffles are brought into their sense of accomplishment. Unfortunately, unlike other instruments, learning songs for the drumkit cannot happen until the student has developed a good sense of rhythm, click (metronome) usage, a good understanding of time signatures and how to count them, and accomplishing Section One. The more advanced a student becomes, the less s/he will rely upon written drum music for the major part of learning.

Songs

For the purpose of enjoyment, every student should learn at least one song every several months. Nothing produces learning music faster than application. They should suggest songs to you, the instructor. You should transcribe them yourself. I **would have** included many song transcriptions in this book that I have personally taught students. However, due to copyright laws, I can only offer those for download for free just not as part of this curriculum (http://udklm.com/song-transcriptions). You will find a series of QR codes on each page where a song is listed. **If you do not have a smart phone** then you cannot use the QR codes. If you do, just download a QR scanner like Qrafter.

Sometimes you need to go off the grid regarding a curriculum. And since there is no exact expectation as to how long each section will take (since each student has different needs), it is best to use your intuition about when s/he may be ready to learn any song. Feel free to move those song requirements around as you need. It mostly depends upon the student. But I have inserted them wherever I personally use them, and where I have found them to be the most successful. And for beginners, I most often don't have the student complete the whole song. The point is to get the student started learning one for the sake of progressing in the instrument, not to beat it into them for three months straight until they get it perfect. Kids love learning. If they feel they are learning, they will stick around. If not, they will likely give up the lessons, and the instrument, thinking it was 'boring.' And that, to me, is a cardinal sin.

Keeping It Real

Learning should be fun, and it most certainly can be. It can be difficult. It can be drudgery sometimes. You, as an instructor, must find that balance and ensure that the student remains interested, learning and excited to have another lesson. I have found that the students who have become frustrated or depressed about their performance have not actually *practiced* per my recommendation (minimum 4 hours per week). When I was a teenager, for years I spent usually three hours a day, upward of 8 hours each day, in practice. When I wasn't practicing music, I was listening to it. My average was about four hours every single day. All I ask is for **four hours a week**. And that should be enough – if used efficiently – to keep the student moving forward. I always ask how much time they spent. If very little time was spent on the material **rarely**, then no big deal. If it becomes a pattern, then the student may receive a sermon somewhere between strong coercion and a light scolding. Whatever it takes. While these students are in your office, studio or home, they are paying *you to keep them motivated and learning*.

Going off the grid

Sometimes you need to go off the grid. By that I mean, *put away the book* and just have fun. Sometimes I turn on the click and help keep their timing straight. Sometimes we play a game of echo where the instructor produces something to be copied by the student. Sometimes I teach musicality with the instrument by having them echo their own ideas (play it once, then try to reproduce it). Sometimes we put it all away and just discuss the problem. *Whatever it takes*. I have been counselor and mentor at times. I suspect most instructors have too if they've been teaching at least a few years.

Use the Website and the Videos!

The website for this book is http://udklm.com - USE IT! It will have all the current links to any and all video content! There are videos for about 90% of all the content in this curriculum. I show you exactly how to play nearly everything. Hint: If you don't yet understand what you are seeing on the video it is because you are not ready for that stage of playing yet. But you **will be**! And when you have acquired the skills, then the videos will make more sense. And you will require the help of your instructor so don't try to jump ahead, thinking that you don't require the basics first. These videos are for the **student and for the parent**! The student will have access to demonstrations (no more smartphone recordings in session!) and the *parent will be able to identify* just what the student should be practicing. If you wish to see all the videos in one location, you can visit the main book website (http://udklm.com) and it will direct you to the correct media site. Occasionally, you will encounter a **QR code** like this: Please use a QR scanner on a smart phone to access the URL.
Go ahead and **test this one.** It will send to the online videos.

As mentioned on the previous page, the website also contains all the song transcriptions (PDF files shared as a free download) used in this curriculum, which were not sold with this book due to copyright restrictions.

Learning By Ear Vs. Sheet Music

An elderly beginner student of mine, after about six lessons (as a part of his retirement package), expressed that he simply did not wish to take the time to learn to read sheet music. He just wasn't interested. Another student in her mid-thirties expressed the same desire. A student who is my age and had been struggling with reading, finally (and somewhat unofficially) surrendered and quit. Another teenage student I taught only once had decided that reading was not what he wanted. He just wanted to play drums. Every single time, every case, the student gives up. It's really understandable. I try to explain that reading is essential, at least a little, in order to progress as far as you desire. Why it is that drummers (especially new ones) believe that drums are not an instrument worthy of site reading is both perplexing and frustrating. If you do not learn to read music, you will invariably hit a ceiling. If you do not take instruction, regardless of your advancement, you will invariably hit a ceiling. If you do not study your instrument deeply, you will invariably flat-line and surrender.

Still, I accommodate when possible, as I must. And like any instrument there are those who learn better by ear, and those who learn better by instruction. I was the former of the two. Though I could read during my youth, I was simply *better* at learning by ear. But in retrospect, that is because *no one bothered to teach me its value*. Had I learned to read, and sought to, I would have progressed ten-fold. During my year at the Atlanta Institute of Music and Media in Duluth, GA, it was foisted upon me like a one hundred pound weight and I bore the challenge. I worked very, very hard. And I overcame my deficiency because I understood its value. Upon leaving the school I was able to chart anything, read anything and just show up at a gig and play if need be. I began to get calls, dozens of them, for my reputation as a short-call drummer, who could "learn" thirty or forty songs at once. Frankly, I wasn't learning them at all! I would show up on a Friday after charting all week, count-off and just *play*. I really don't need to know the material, although it helps. How absolutely liberating! There is simply no way to learn that many songs in a week. I have learned highly complex material and done studio-recorded videos – all from learning by reading. What's more, I not have (to date) over 750 well-organized charts that I can pull out at any time if I get a call for a gig. The more I chart, the less I have to.

On the other hand, students have the prerogative to determine what direction they wish to take. But I do not advise learning by ear *alone.* With emphasis, ear-only learning should accompany chart learning. After all, music is a language. And drumming is a way of speaking it. You can learn to speak by emersion but you will never speak the language well until you can read and write it.

"*Well, I just think that a drummer should* feel *the music.*" And I agree. There is no dichotomy between reading and feeling the music once you become fluent. I hear the same argument when it comes to a click/metronome. But's that argument is simply Oscar Mayar Kraft Brand Bologna. Try reading anything in a language you are just learning and of course it will sound stiff, clunky and awkward. But in your own tongue reading is a form of expression that you mostly do not need to think about. It goes the same for any instrument. **All instruments require reading for fluency** and drumming is no different. An exceptional reader will perform so eloquently that you would never know s/he was reading the whole time. Most of the masters of this instrument *all read music* to some degree. As an example, Vinnie Colaiuta got his start with Frank Zappa by *reading* some of the most difficult material conceivable during his audition. He got that gig and is now one of the most sought-after drummers in the world.

More importantly, as an instructor, I tell the following to any student who proposes to bypass reading, "*Well, I can certainly teach you to train your ear. But that is only one aspect of drumming. I simply cannot teach you* how *to do things when it gets complicated if you cannot read it.*" Things get really complex in drumming. If you cannot see the 15-syllable Icelandic word, pronouncing it will be far more difficult. In other words, if you want the short route then I'm not your guy. But what I prefer, and what this book is designed to do, is to teach the student the *art of drumming* and how to speak the language of music with the drumkit. I hope you'll take the time to learn it. Nothing comes easy. Hard work pays off. And the end result is your own love of the instrument, and the joy of performing.

B) Technique, Stick Grip and Pedal Control

The discussion of foot technique has been, at best, non-descript. After all the drumkit as a backing instrument has only been in existence since around 1910 (I am purposefully discounting the full history of the "trap" kit, which reached into the mid-eighteenth century as an orchestral instrument). Given that the drumkit is so relatively new, and that the modern kick pedal was not fully developed until later on, it is easy to understand why the subject is so amorphous. As the instrument progresses, the more instruction advances, the more concise the explanations will become. I hope to play some small part in that process.

Foot technique and methods have been handed down from one instructor to the next for the last one hundred years. Like the actual notation of drumkit music itself, there never seemed to be a decisive set of right or wrong instructions. With that in mind, my purpose here is to provide an overview of every possible technique, indicating how they are used, when they are used, and in what musical style. The short of the lesson I hope the reader will take from this is, *there is no right or wrong foot technique*, but there are many that you should adopt. The technique I most often use (heel-toe) is far different than what others use, and that works quite well for me. However, *I use all of these techniques*. And I would expect my students to do the same. Every technique has a specific purpose.

As a side note, most of the techniques used on the kick drum pedal can also be used on the hi-hat pedal. There will be a few more tips for the hi-hat pedal in a later section.

General learning tips

There is always an adjustment period when learning a new technique. Go slow. Take your time. Be patient. The method I teach is mainly what I call the "one beat at a time" method – muscle memory is key to learning everything in drumming. This means, "**stop, see, study, strike**." And, ironically, the faster you attempt a new skill, the longer it will take you to learn it. Learn each beat (however many notes there are **on** that beat) then go to the next beat *a-rhythmically*. Meaning, do not attempt to create a rhythm until the muscle memory is there. This works every time for virtually everything you will ever learn. You will increase speed and control without thinking about it. Then you will know it at *all* speeds.

Stomp method

In all cases, *never use the upper thigh muscles!* You will find that the *stomp method*, as it is impolitely dubbed, will cause you only grief, pain, sluggishness, loss of balance and a lack of control. Lifting the leg using the upper leg muscles is the **only incorrect way** to strike the kick drum with the pedal. You will feel a tug at your body, throwing you either backward or forward, and soreness at the hip, and utter discomfort at higher speeds. Most early students either start off this way or fall into it at some point.

Six basic techniques

There are six basic ways to attack the kick drum using the pedal. All pedals function the same in this regard, whether long board or short, whether chain driven or belt or camshaft driven. I will discuss each technique in the pages that follow. There are two different landings of the beater: buried and free/open. **Buried** is when the beater remains on the drumhead. It creates a shortened sound. **Free** is when the beater bounces back away from the head and allows the drumhead to resonate. Both are useful. Learn both. Resting the ball of the foot after any stroke of the beater will "open" the sound by removing the beater from the drumhead. Continued pressure will "close" the sound by burying the beater into the drumhead, as aforementioned. This is true of all the techniques.

For illustrations, turn to the pages following this section entitled, *Foot Position Diagrams*.

1. Ankle only	2. Toe only
3. Toe-to-ball drop	4. Heel-swing
5. Toe-heel slide	6. Heel-toe

1. **Ankle Only**

Use only the ankle for speed and versatility. If you want 250bpm double-kick speed, this is the way to do it. Although, it does not work so well for slower speeds. Ensure you are not leaning into your throne. If you lift your feet you should not fall over. Balance is key. The heel will come slightly off the pedal board, supported by the ball of the foot. Only the ankle moves. Again, this is for higher speeds so practicing this slowly can be tricky. Simply use the calve muscles to hold up the heel above the pedal. Lift the heel about a centimeter; now drop the *toe and ball* of the foot as a strike. Eventually you will increase speed. Some drummers combine this with the swivel technique (#4).

The other method is the reverse, which I often call the *twitch*. Simply twitch or quiver your foot up and down like you would when nervous or antsy. Everyone has done it. Start at a higher speed to figure out how this technique works. Eventually you will build the required muscles for control. Use both methods to learn this technique.

2. **Toe Only (heel down)**

Used only for light playing for music like soft ballads, jazz, bossa nova, et cetera, there is *no power* in this technique. But it is required for soft playing. This is one way that beginner students naturally use the kick pedal, the stomp method being the other.

Simply rest the heel on the pedal board and lift the toe. It is really that simply and doesn't require any special instruction. Again, use *only for light music or low volume performances*. You will use this technique often when applied properly.

3. **Toe-to-ball Drop**

A bit more difficult to explain, this is technique is used for both speed and power. It is a common method used throughout performers in jazz, rock, fusion and gospel – really, anything that requires high-speed single pedal footwork.

Start with the heel up as high as you can lift it, the toe touching the top of the pedal board. Now drop the heel but land on the ball of the foot. The impact of the ball of the foot should create the strike of the beater to the drumhead. It is the drop that creates the impact. *Do not slide* the foot. The toe will remain where it began at the top of the pedal board. This technique is used often in the samba style (uh-1, uh-2, uh-3, uh-4).

4. **Heel-Swing (swivel)**

This is a side-side motion, and is perhaps the least common and most difficult to learn. It has its place. It is not used for power, but comfort and rhythm and speed. I use it on the hi-hat foot often, and sometimes during a "four on the floor" (quarter note) kick drum pattern where I will swing the foot side to side for the purpose of rhythm keeping. The heels may perform this independently using hi-hat and kick drum pedal. But with double-kick pedals this becomes complex. And as aforementioned, it is used also in combination with the "ankle only" technique.

Begin by swinging (swiveling) your right foot from side to side with the heel up and ball of the foot down. This will create a light impact, a bit louder than the toe-only method. You may swing both feet in the same direction for double-kick, or opposing directions. But either one will take time.

5. **Toe-Heel Slide**

This is a very common kick drum pedal technique. Similar to the "toe-to-ball drop," the heel begins higher up than the "ankle only" technique, then dropping the heel, allowing gravity to land it firmly on the pedal for the strike.

The two differences are: a) the ball of the foot begins at the bottom of the footboard; b) then slides upward toward the kick drumhead. I rarely use this method, as it is somewhat inaccurate. Many drummers use it for a quick 32nd note "double" hit where a 16th note would go. Again, slide the foot upward. The first strike is when the heel hits the footboard. The second strike is when the ball of the foot slides and strikes the top of the footboard.

6. **Heel-Toe**

The popularity of this technique is growing as drummers become more aware of its versatility, simplicity and balance for the body. The punch delivery comes from both strikes: heel and then ball of the foot (not technically the toes). Jared Falk (drumeo.com) in "Bass Drum Secrets" first introduced this technique to me in 2007. I spent upwards of three hours at a time on double-kick pedals working this out. It requires, and will build, stronger muscles on the sides of the shin and from the calve area. It takes months to integrate this technique into your daily playing, hours and hours of devotion, and years before you stop thinking about it while drumming. But the payoff is tremendous. Being able to perform very accurate and tight 32nd or 64th notes with one foot is a real asset. Applied consistently to double-kick pedals, you will soon join the "200 club" (200 BPM) for double kick. The drawback is that it often requires a "buried beater," which will deaden the sound of the kick drumhead. There is a way to back off the beater after the strike, but it takes practice.

To perform this technique, simply rock the foot back and forth from the heel to the ball (toe) while applying pressure to both. Both the heel and toe strikes should resonate at equal volume if executed correctly. Practice this no *slower* than about 80bpm. It was not intended to provide 32nd notes much slower than that. The technique simply will not work.

You will *need to tighten the tension* on your pedal. For a spring pedal, get one of the high-tension springs for a few dollars at your local music store. Tighten it nearly all the way to the maximum tension. It will feel awkward and restrictive and clumsy at first. You may realize just how much your muscles have been in need of some exercise! John Blackwell, though he doesn't use this technique, tightens his all the way to the maximum to practice ankle-only, as do most speed metal players.

Again, you will need to practice this technique *a lot* and for *very long periods* at once in order for it to become natural. Then, you will need to adjust your entire playing style in order to accommodate it! But I tell you with conviction that, if you are serious about the drums, it is well worth the time investment and energy. Just keep trying.

Pedal Tips

The mechanics of how the foot and pedal work together is as complex as it is simple: What works for you may not work for others. The same philosophy of "*don't overthink it*" applies. This is because the foot is a highly complex piece of machinery. There are 26 bones (about ¼ of the 206 bones in your body), 33 joints, 20 differently functioning muscles and over 100 tendons and ligaments… in just one foot. Each pedal has at least, on average, 15 working parts. Each foot and each pedal have hundreds of varieties. Is it any wonder why there is no exact science to foot technique? Ask any professional (full time) drummer about their technique and you will only be shown what *they* do.

All that said, I could perhaps provide some tips on how to maximize use of your kick pedal, and some techniques. In all cases, remember that *relaxation is the key* to unlocking speed and endurance. There should be zero tension in your upper legs. Here is a short list of considerations when discovering what pedal works best for you:

Pedal

1. Spring tension
2. Footboard length and angle, split or single
3. Beater type, angle and height
4. Kick drumhead tension and type
5. Pedal drive (cam, chain or belt)

Body

6. Muscles and arch design
7. Balance and seat position: thigh placement, height of throne
8. Foot placement (where is it natural for your feet to fall)
9. Angle of your thighs (hips should be slightly raised above the knees)
10. Natural and unnatural defects (e.g., MLS or car-accident therapy)

There are likely many more considerations for both body and for pedal. Again, there is no science. It comes down to what works best for your body. But please wear proper footwear. I use water shoes. No Boots!

A RELAXED GRIP

One of the more difficult aspects of drumming to teach is that the stick grip is not rigid. It is not tense. It is not tight. The tighter the stick is held the less vibrational quality it has, the less sonic reverberation it delivers to the drumhead, the less dexterity and agility the drummer will have. I have had to correct students who were taught by their prior instructor to "gorilla grip" the stick using the index finger and thumb (fingers 1 & 2). What this effectively does is restrict the movement of the stick, creates a tense delivery, forces the wrist to overwork, stunts skill-growth and generally creates bad visuals.

Taught to me personally by Dave Weckl and Tom Knight at the Atlanta Institute of Music and Media, and what is found in nearly every classically trained or high-level drummer, is to hold the stick in the "pistol grip," where the index finger (finger 2) points toward the end of the stick, or toward the drum itself, in a relaxed fashion (see figure 1). I have also heard this called "core grip" referring to drum and bugle corps. Another advantage to this grip is not putting the knuckle in jeopardy of being struck against the snare! Admittedly, this method took me nearly a year to fully incorporate into my drumming (after 33+ years of doing it the wrong way)! Hopefully, it will not take you as long. If you are a new student then start using grip this now! For a while it will seem as though the stick is going to get away from you. And for a time, it just may. I can attest to many times missing my target or coming up to hit a cymbal from below and losing the stick during that transitional period. Be patient. Learn to fail, for each failure is a step toward success. Eventually, it will become comfortable and normal and you will feel your drumming begin to open up immensely.

Figure 1

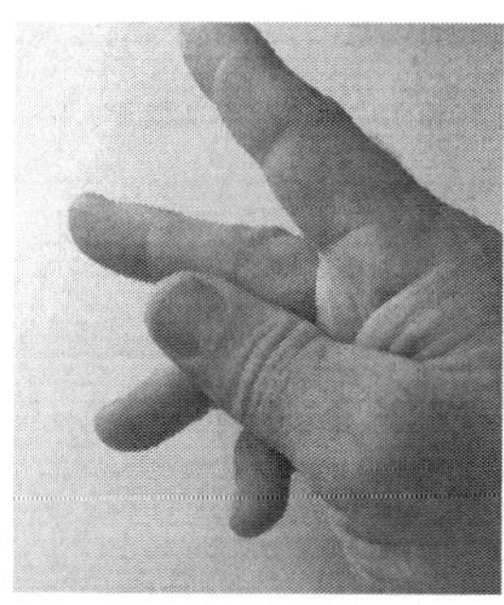

To properly grip the stick, place the middle finger (finger #3) at the middle knuckle, together with the thumb (finger #1), as the pivot point of the stick. Without the stick, the middle knuckle of the middle finger should be against the thumb. This is the fulcrum of the stick where it will pivot. This will create the aforementioned "pistol grip" where the finger is pointing like a gun.

The number one problem I encounter with new students trying to learn this grip is *over-thinking* the grip. Yet, it is perhaps the most simplistic and *natural* grip possible. How I explain it is, imagine you are going to throw the stick. Go ahead. Grab it. Hoist it like you are going to throw it a hundred yards. Next, move the stick slowly as if it were being thrown (don't let go!). Look at your *natural* grip. This is not only the precise way you will strike the drum (to be discussed later); your index finger (finger #2) is now pointing at your target naturally. Just relax the hand. Another indicator is to grab the stick from your hand (or someone else can). If it slid out easily, your grip is fine. I ask students to grab the stick from my hand after I play a few seconds on any drum. It should slide right out. They usually laugh with surprise. No tension. That is the objective.

There are two major stick grips: Traditional and Matched. Within the matched grip, there are two sub-grips: French and German. However, a proper strike of *any grip* will require a "whipping motion" as if either throwing the stick or whipping a towel. This motion first moves the shoulder, then the elbow, then the wrist then the fingers, then the stick, in that order. The instructor will need to demonstrate this to the student.

Traditional Grip

The history of this grip begins before the advent of the drumset (even before the orchestral drumkit in the 18th century). Field drummers in the British Army (and in the American Revolution army following that) were the progenitors of this grip. The marching drum for the field drummer was on the left hip with the head of the drum pointed forward. This forced the left hand to be held in a slanted fashion. As time progressed and the snare drum became popular, it was propped on a chair to the left of the drummer, pointed toward the drumkit. Jazz inherited this playing style in the 1920's. Transitioning to a traditional grip can be a bit for someone accustomed only to matched grip. If you choose this as a main grip, you will need to setup your entire kit around it. If you do not, you will simply not be able to effectively use it. Choose one and master it: traditional or matched. If you choose to learn both matched and traditional (advised!) There are a few ways to "flip" between traditional and matched grips using the left hand. Ask your instructor to demonstrate these two you after you have mastered both grips.

Figure 2

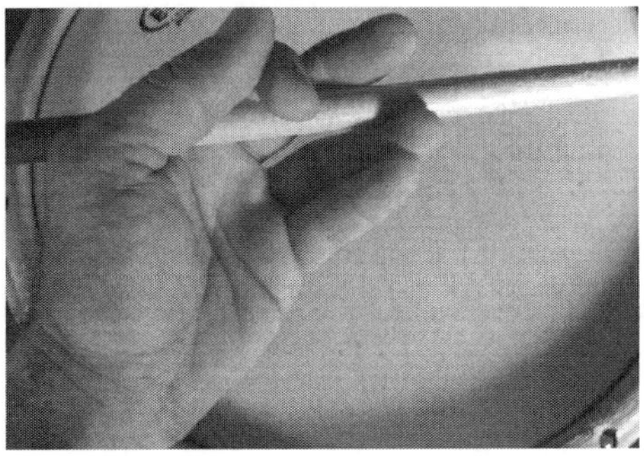

To achieve a traditional grip, use the *left hand*. Even if you are left-handed, most kits are right-handed. You will severely hamper your ability to play other drummers' drumkits if you do not use your left hand for traditional grip.

Allow the stick in the left hand to rest in the pocket between the thumb and index finger. The fulcrum will be between the thumb and index finger (#1 & #2) and rest firmly in that pocket. This is an open-handed traditional grip (a technique you will use in a more advanced stage of playing). Next, the stick will slide between fingers 3 & 4 and will rest between the first and second knuckles. Keep the palm facing sideways. *The palm should never face entirely upward* or the wrist will work too hard and limit your speed and power.

Matched Grip: French

The matched grip requires both hands to look the same. That is, both hands must *function the same*. The best way to do this is to "mirror" your hands during any exercise, which will be discussed later in this book.

Figure 3

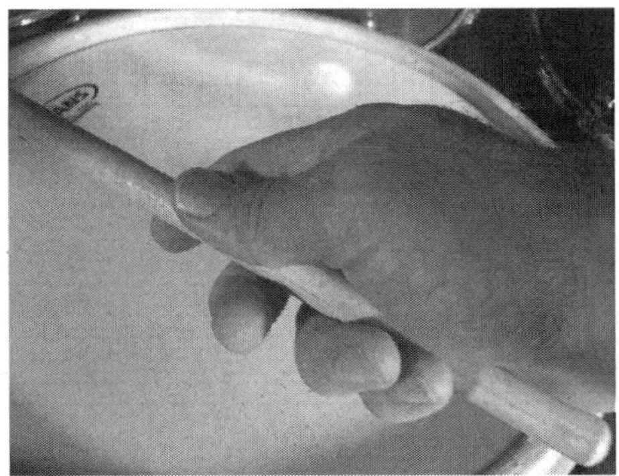

The **French grip** was developed for the purpose of playing in a relaxed fashion, with more use of the fingers than wrists. Of course, the drawback is slightly less power than the **German grip**. But it creates a great deal of finesse and facilitates smoother playing. Most classic and highly skilled drummers use this grip. Various techniques will require this grip in the future. You *need to learn this grip*, as well as German grip.

Figure 4

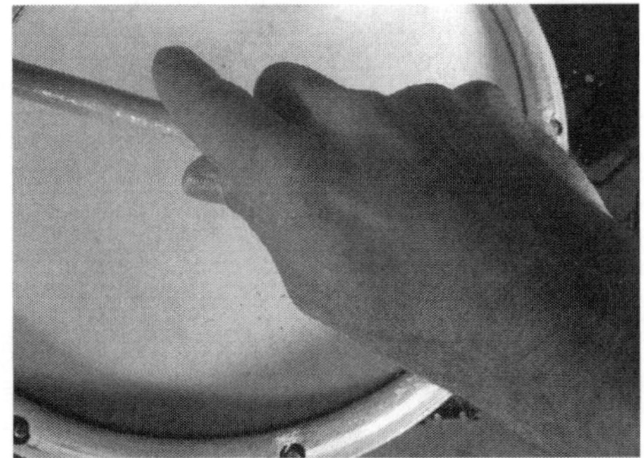

The main rule with this grip is that both thumbs should be facing upward, palms sideways (figure 3). The thumb and middle finger still pivot the stick. However, be sure not to allow the stick to slide in between the thumb and index; the stick should rest underneath the thumb. **Mainly**, keep the thumb *parallel* to the stick as much as possible and use more *finger* than wrist action.

Matched Grip: German

Hold the sticks so that both thumbs are facing one another, palms down (figure 4). This grip will provide more power in the strike of the drum. The stick will still pivot between fingers 1 & 3, but come upward *toward* the pocket between fingers 1 & 2. Again, attempt to throw the stick (without releasing it). You will see where it naturally pivots. Your instructor may need to demonstrate this to you. Fingers create the speed. *The smaller the muscles, the faster the strike can be.* Also, getting *both hands to learn the same skills equally* is paramount to creating speed. A key to understanding these grips is, there should be little to no "air" or "space" between the stick and the palm of the hand. When the stick moves you should feel it strike against the palm.

Cross Sticking

Although it is not technically a "grip," the *cross stick* does require somewhat of an alternate grip. The purpose of the cross stick (X-stick) is to create a softer, more precise backbeat in a rhythm, or a "click." It is often used in Latin, Cuban, African, Jazz, Country, and ballads … but is also used in virtually every other style of music to some degree.

Figure 5

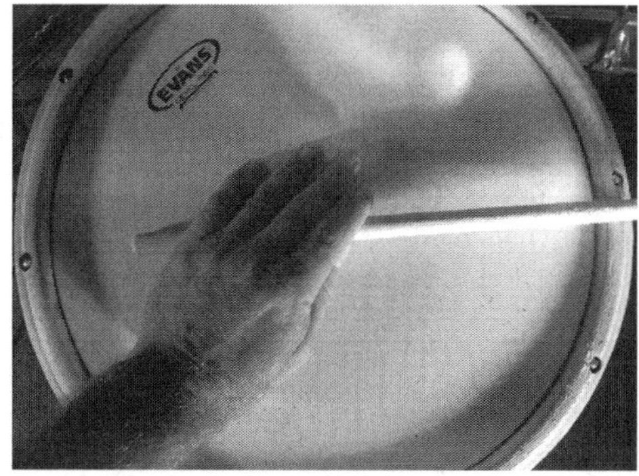

The butt of the stick should be approximately an inch from the hoop of the snare. The front of the stick rests over the hoop on the opposite side, but placement will alter the sound as required. The palm will ordinarily remain down on the head of the drum (with exception!), with fingers across the stick (figure 5) to mute the snare head.

Figure 6

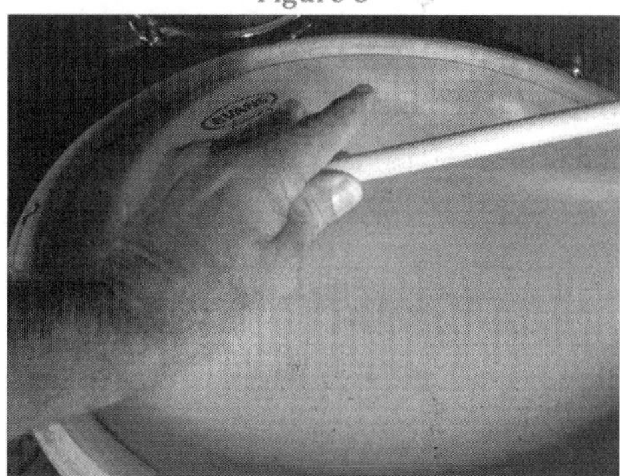

To strike with the stick, keep the palm down and lift with the remaining fingers (figure 6).

This grip (or technique) is represented on drum sheet music as "x" on the "c" treble line almost universally in every corner of the music world. The "x" means "cross." Become familiar and accustomed to using this grip. You will be using it not only in this curriculum but also in every facet of drumming in your future.

C) Foot Positions Diagrams

1 ankle only (a)

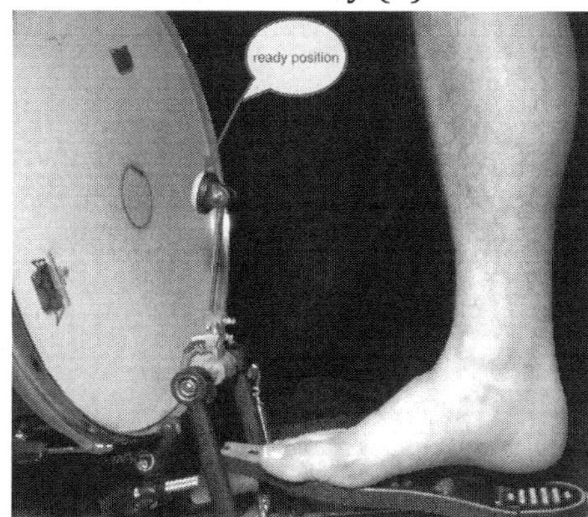
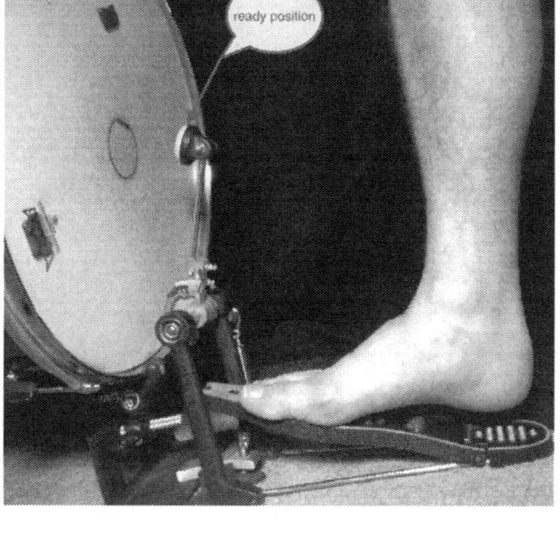

1 ankle only (b)

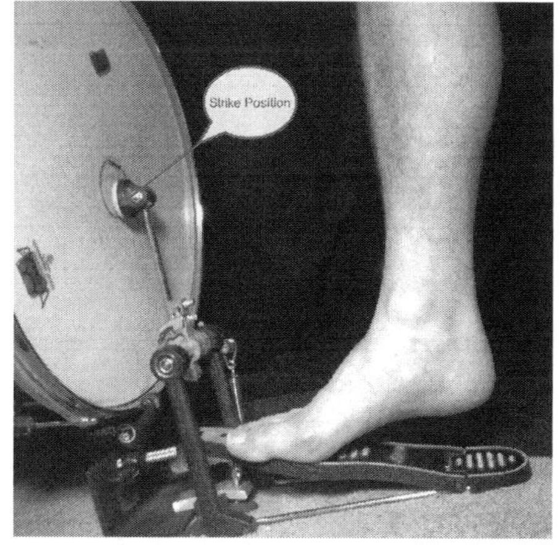

2 toe only (a)

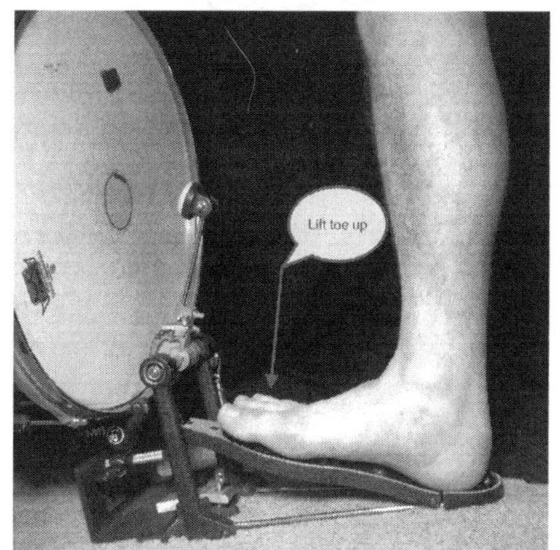

2 toe only (b)

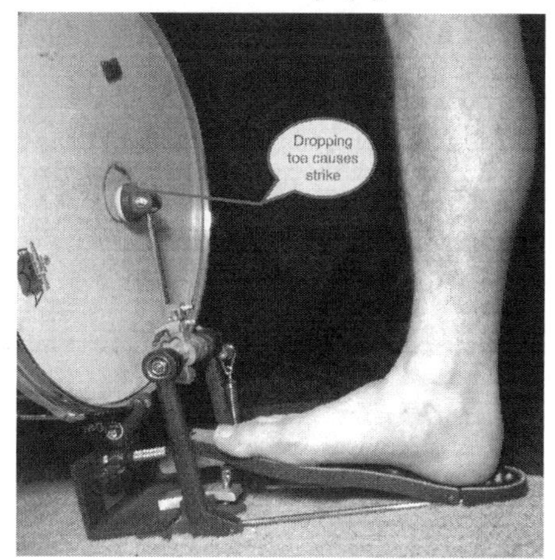

3 toe-to-ball drop (a)

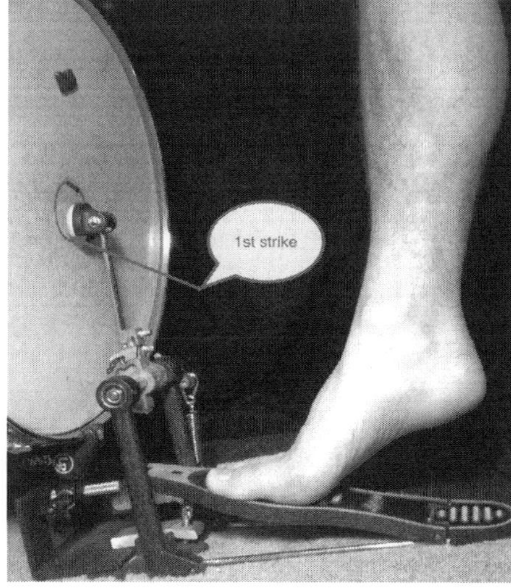

3 toe-to-ball drop (b)

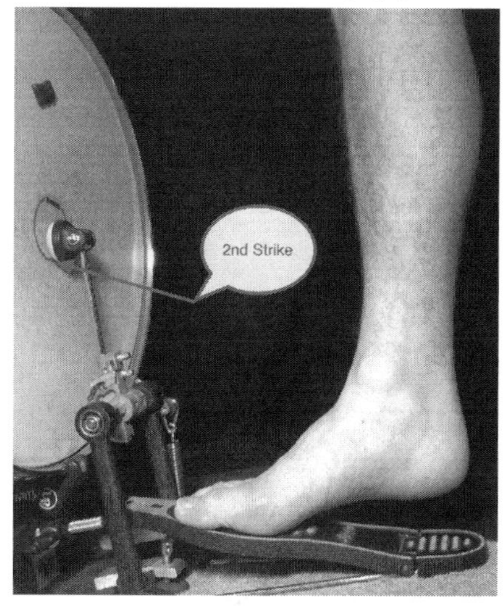

4 heel-swing (a)

4 heel-swing (b)

5 toe-heel slide (a)

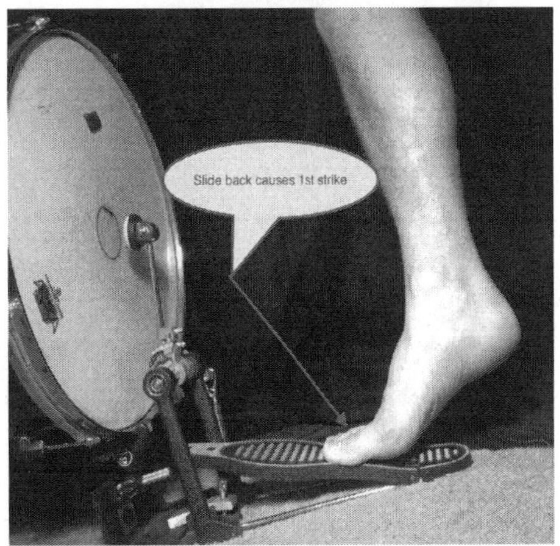

5 toe-heel slide (b)

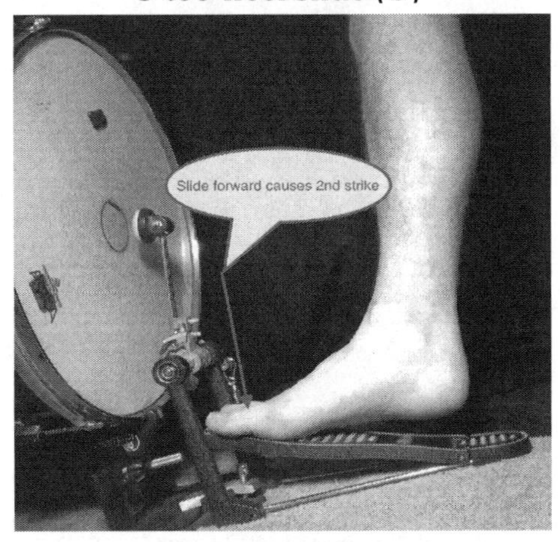

6 heel-toe (a)

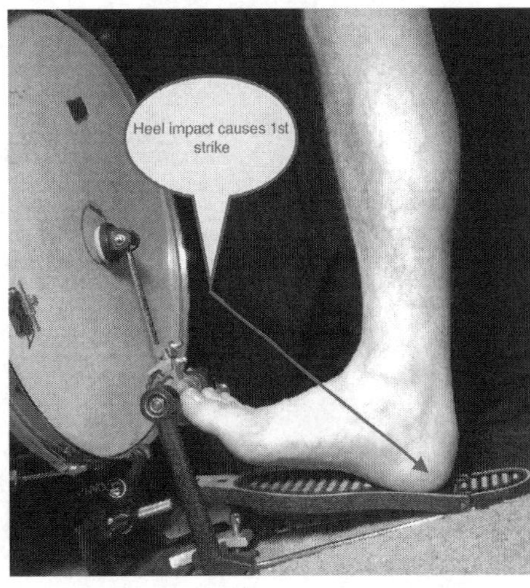

6 heel-toe (b)

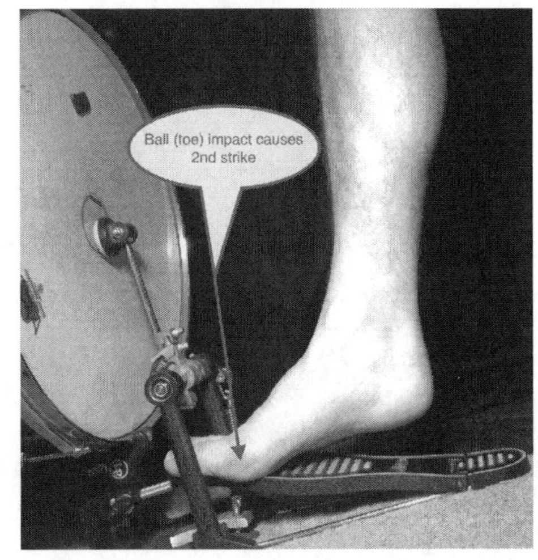

D) Hi-Hat Pedal Techniques

It is time to discuss something rarely covered in drumming how-to books: the use of the hi-hat foot. It is somewhat of a non-discussed art. For the most part, you either observed and learned it or you didn't. I know of some instructors that have thankfully pressed on about it, and I'm certain there are others. But I've not seen anything written on the subject, so I'll discuss it here since I teach these things to my students.

Time Keeping with the Hi-Hat Foot

The hi-hat foot, as often as possible, should *always remain in motion* even when unheard. Time can be kept with the hi-hat foot with a simple undetected "bounce" where the foot bounces like a little dancer without raising the hi-hat pedal; it can be used in "splash" mode, opening up the sound for the band; a basic toe/ball method to provide succinct eighth and quarter notes to keep the band on track (on any beat) or some combination. These can be used in virtually every drumming situation.

There are certainly some who disagree with me on the idea that it should always be in motion, and that the hi-hat foot is an integral part of the drumming experience. But those drummers often haven't tried it because they haven't learned to value it. Or perhaps they tried only briefly and found it too much learning for its value. Yet, you must acquire the skill if you plan on keeping solid time (something at which we are all imperfect), if you want to build your level of coordination and interdependence, and if you like keeping the band in time (and the audience aware of where you are!) during a solo section. It also creates a great sound if used properly and can add wonders to your overall presentation. Virtually everything I play includes the hi-hat foot. Did it take a long time to become habitual? Not much – a few years. But long-suffering pays off when it comes to any instrument. Keep at it and it will become natural to you. The *Kick Drum Reading Exercises* (1 & 2) in this book will get you moving that direction. Stick with those exercises and it will move quickly for you.

Time keeping is the major purpose of the hi-hat foot. But it also completes the drumming experience for both the drummer and for the audience, and keeps the band straight. Whenever I'm pointed at for a solo (go!) during a performance, especially when "comp'ed" (meaning "accompanied" by other musicians), I attempt to keep time using various techniques with the hi-hat foot.

The other major reason behind using your hi-hat foot is … it's *part of the instrument!* It sounds cool when done tastefully, with good reason and forethought. Though taste, reason and forethought cannot really be taught in a book (and shouldn't be), the ways in which the hi-hat is used *can be* taught. Please consider the following methods and techniques for the hi-hat foot. Though there may be other possibilities, these are the main ideas.

Heel-Swing

As taught in the chapter on *Technique, Stick Grip and Pedal Control* in this book, this method is a side-side motion. Its purpose is comfort and rhythm. Please see the *Foot Positions Diagrams* page for visual instruction. I use it at times when I'm bored behind the kit to give me something else constructive to think about. It doesn't create any special sounds, but assists in a good solid groove. To produce this fun effect, swivel the heel back and forth while leaving the ball of the foot on the pedal. The extremes of the movement should create a small "clap" sound of the hi-hat.

Ankle Only

This is used for speed. If you want to produce, for instance, triplets on each foot (rrr-lll) or doubles (rr-ll), then this is the way to do that with the hi-hat pedal. The heel will come slightly of the pedal board, supported by the ball of the foot. Only the ankle moves.

Splash/Heel-Toe

I use this as frequently as I can get away with it. It fills up the sound. This is actually the heel-toe method used on the kick drum pedal. The heel creates the open splash; the ball/toe closes the hi-hat. The accent, of course, is on the opened hi-hat splash sound. When learning this technique try using the splash on the downbeats, and on the upbeats for variations. When using an upbeat on the ride bell, go with a downbeat on the splash, and vice-versa.

Stomp Method!

Please don't hate me for sounding contradictory. I would never recommend this for any other reason than simple sound effects purposes, and not for extended periods. Sometimes splashing the hi-hat in a consistent eight-note pattern sounds just explosively good. Just don't keep it up for long. It's exhausting, unbalancing and intrusive to the music if used inappropriately. Simply push quickly at the pedal to produce a splash and lift the foot completely off the pedal again. Repeat.

Toe Only

Mostly used in jazz on the 2 & 4 as part of the general time keeping (ride and hi-hat are the time keeping mechanisms in jazz drumming), and some light bossa or ballads, *toe only* is meant only for very light drumming, soft music and cocktail gigs.

Bouncing Foot

Sometimes the hi-hat foot just needs *move*. Sometimes, it's just not about the sound, but about the internal aspect of drumming – always having a beat resonating in our heads with or without music. At times you just want to keep the time *for yourself* and not let anyone hear it. Other times you'll want to accent only *sometimes* using the hi-hat, even with continual motion. For instance, when playing a samba rhythm (1, a2, a3, a4) with the kick drum pedal, the hi-hat pedal will always play the "&" of the beat. In doing so, eventually, you will find that the foot naturally bounces in between "&" on all the eight notes. It only *plays* the "&" but continues moving on the #'s as well. It's natural to do this, and forcing it lends to unnecessary complication. If you wish to generate this rhythmic effect, keep it in mind but try not to force it – don't think about it. The more you force it, the more it will frustrate you.

Luminous Sound Effects

Although not within the realm of time keeping, sometimes a drummer will splash or "clap" the hi-hat as part of a fill or rhythm. Try an alternating splash and hi tom combination or the low-toms and a splash in unison. Remember that there are no rules. Do what your creative mind drives you to do. Do not limit yourself in any way. Be Creative.

E) Steps To Learning Any Rhythm

I teach all my students that there are two basic ways to learn any drumkit rhythm: 1) one *beat* at a time; or 2) *layering*. It is important to note that not everyone works the same. Each student (including you) is designed to learn differently. Some learn by watching and mimicking, some by reading and reproducing, some by some variation of both instruction and self-study. I have been most successful using either of these two methods.

EZ Time Signatures

Although *written* music has been around at latest since 1457 (Mainz psalter), or earliest the 10th century (Guido of Arezzo), musical instructors at every level *still find it difficult* to explain the simple time signature. There seems to be so many boorish and convoluted ways to explain a time signature (4/4 or 7/8 or 15/16) that it leaves the student with the sense that the instructor either doesn't understand it his/herself or it's so vastly complex that it is not worth understanding. For students who have previously been taught the time signature, when I ask them to explain it, generally they lose all coherencies and seem to forget Standard English. I'm not being harsh on the student, not whatsoever; the student can understand only as well as the instructor teaches. There is no need to create a YouTube video. There is no need to put it on a whiteboard. There is no need to take ten minutes to explain it. When I teach the concept to new students *of any age* or experience, the light bulb goes on in no later than 60 seconds. If I drill them on it, they understand it. It *really is that easy* to understand. It really is this simple:

> "*4/4 means there are four quarter notes in a measure.*" And then I follow up with, "*6/8 means there are six eighth notes in a measure.*" Then I ask, "*So, what does 9/16 mean?*" And the student usually gets it. "*9/16 means there are nine sixteenth notes in a measure.*" And such is the most uncomplicated way to explain it.

How Many
What Kind

… And now, the steps to learning a rhythm (in any time signature):

One Beat At A Time

Muscle Memory is the name of the game. It is the basis of learning any drumset rhythm (or *anything* requiring coordination), and likely any complex instrument under the Sun. Learning material slowly may seem counter-intuitive at first. It may seem to you that learning something *at the speed you plan on playing it* would be the most practical thing to do. However, following the prescription of *play slow first* will create a relaxed, confident, smooth performance that will naturally speed up. As with martial arts, learning a skill slowly will create a smooth motion, which will create a better understanding of the motion, which will create speed (slow = smooth = fast). I have learned most of the highly complex fusion material, and some transcribed complex drum fills (Gary Novak!) and even full drum solos this way. Anything can be taught to someone who has the patience to learn a particular rhythm. When students get caught up in the same mistake over and over, which I often purposely allow, I ask them to stop at the precise beat where the mistake persists and *only then* continue – *a-rhythmically.*

That is, don't try to keep it in rhythm. Just get the muscle memory correct. And in about three to five passes, the problem is gone. When learning one beat at a time, you play *all notes* on that beat. Again, d*o not attempt to make a rhythm* at this point. Just create muscle memory. In time, you will naturally speed up and begin playing it rhythmically.

Layering Beats

To "layer" a rhythm you will learn it *rhythmically*, which is the opposite approach to *one beat at a time*. Layering requires that you learn one "voice" (one sound) using one limb (hand/foot) at a time. Some rhythms will require this method, some the other. You will decide which works best for you as the student or the instructor.

In layering a rhythm, for instance, play just the ride bell part. Then continue repeating it as an ostinato (a continuous rhythm). Then add another voice to the mix. Continue this until the rhythm comes together.

I advise using the following procedure to layer a *complex* rhythm:

1) Kick drum only
2) RH + RF
3) LH + RF
4) LF + RF
5) RH + LH
6) RH + LF
7) LH + LF
8) ALL together

The reason this works is that it joins together all the possible combinations of limbs. In most scenarios you will not need to do this. But as an example, when learning the sections in this book entitled, "*Kick Drum Reading Exercise #1 (8th notes)*" or "*Kick Drum Reading Exercise #2 (16th notes)*," this method will come in very handy. Like a pianist learns one hand at a time, you will learn one limb at a time, then combine them.

F) Tips for Parents:

Help Your Child Succeed in their Music Lessons

"*How can I help my child succeed in music*?"

Here are a few ideas to improve the learning experience for you and your child, which can directly impact your child's success with that instrument.

Encouragement Prevents Discouragement

First, help your child understand that learning any instrument is a long-term process that includes some challenges and it is normal for your child to feel discouraged from time to time. Let your child know that proper dedication to practice in the early stages of learning a musical instrument can yield years of enjoyment. When your child faces those challenges from time to time, avoid the simple response, "*Just keep working on it and it will get better...*" and certainly don't belittle them. Instead, do your best to understand the issue causing their struggle.

A couple things to consider – the predicament might not be caused by lack of effort or dedication; improper technique might be the culprit and additional input from their instructor might be required. Practicing with an improper technique can diminish the student's progress and make learning music very discouraging. But, there will be times when your child just doesn't (or you don't) feel like practicing. When that happens, give them a day or two off. Just like you and me, your child may need a little break once in a while. It is most important to encourage your child throughout their struggles and allow them to be a part of the solution.

Don't Push

Learning an instrument should be fun. The child (or you) chose to learn this instrument because s/he was excited about playing it. If it becomes cumbersome, overly difficult, or produces negative feelings too often, the student will no longer want to play, and will no longer practice. If you feel like your student (or you) is getting uninspired it is either due to a lack of practice, or due to burnout. It begins as a brownout. Flickers of stress fly and then … try to catch it before it becomes blackout. Lay off the gas awhile.

Prevent having an Overworked Family

A lot of parents live as unpaid, professional chauffeurs. They work really hard to drive their kid to games in the summer, lessons year round, school events like plays and musicals, sleep-overs, park visits, family outings … and in all their excitement to do all this for their kid, as glad as they are to do it … the child is just plain exhausted and no longer having fun. I would rather have a student fully attentive than to have an exhausted one fighting sleep while I teach. For this reason, if a parent is pushing their child too hard, I will have to break the news that the student is simply not making any progress. If it's baseball, please finish baseball and then come back. If it's a musical, please finish the musical and then come back. Student retention numbers mean nothing to me if the students are not learning. As a parent of five kids myself, I know the struggle between wanting to do for your kids and wanting to have a sane family. Choose the latter. If you are serious about you or your child learning an instrument, remember that it takes *energy*, *dedication* and *isolation*. Learn to allow breathing room in your lives.

Make a Schedule and Stick To It

Interest or not, love for the instrument or no, the student will languish without a regimented, and expected, time and comfortable place to practice. There are any number of ways to make this happen given our busy lifestyles: 1) set a timer if your schedule allows it; 2) set reminders and post-it notes; 3) once in awhile push him/her to "*just spend ten minutes on it – don't worry about the assignment. Just have fun*." Usually, it will be much longer; 4) ____________________ <Your idea here>.

Just remember, that it should be fun, but it must be a discipline or the student will cease to progress. The instructor doesn't get inspired. The student loses hope. The parent feels like it's wasted money, time and energy. On the other hand, a practiced student is an inspired one. S/he will be excited to make more progress. The instructor will be inspired. You will be inspired. And you will be proud. But discipline and regimen is the key.

Learn Together

"*Is my child progressing at the proper rate*?" Don't be overly concerned with your child's initial progress because the basics of music can be initially difficult. Acquiring proper finger strength and dexterity coupled with learning other skills are enough to make any grown man struggle.

One step that has yielded terrific results is having the parent(s) **participate in their child's music lesson**. This not only allows the parent to better understand their child's progress, it benefits their child during the lesson and can provide a sound basis for the parent to assist their child with practice at home. As a busy parent, it is tough to remain at your child's side during practice, but if you spend 30 minutes several times a week working with them, you will drastically improve your child's ability to succeed in music.

Dedicated Practice Space and Time

Having a dedicated time and distraction-free practice space can support productive practice sessions. It is best to use a location without a television or video games. Create a musically inspirational practice space that includes the necessary tools – chair without armrests, music stand, metronome, pencil, notepad, and proper lighting. Then, add some inspiration with musical pictures or posters. Make it their space. Do what you can.

Timing Matters

Don't forget the metronome. Practicing with a metronome or a click track aids your child's development of good rhythm. All too often I receive new students with poor rhythm skills because they neglected to utilize a metronome or some sort of click track while learning the basics. Many students believe practicing drills and scales slowly doesn't require using a metronome. But nothing could be further from the truth. It is difficult maintain proper rhythm when practicing slowly because of the extended gaps between notes. And by all means *practice to the music track* whenever possible.

G) The First Drumset

Most drum instructors have been consulted as to what drumset equipment a new student should have. If you do not yet have a drumset and are looking, my most valuable advice to you is to *start small.* Don't go big. You want to buy something used, and preferably from a store to which you can return anything that doesn't work. But before the drumset, and above all else get a **practice pad!** A 12" neoprene-coated drum pad is perfect. It would be wise to invest in a **music stand** also.

Gear

You (or your child) will need a minimum of the following components:

- Throne (seat) – something swivel adjustable. Avoid the "notch" thrones.
- Kick drum – nothing smaller than 20" in diameter, preferably 22."
- Kick drum pedal – anything for a beginner will be fine.
- Hi-Hat stand – three legged
- Hi-Hat Cymbals
- Snare drum – eight lugs will do, ten is better; preferably 14" diameter, 5.5" depth.
- Snare stand – the "cradle" should hold the snare snug and not wobble.

Again, those are the *absolute basic* minimum requirements.

If you desire and can afford a little more than that, you may also consider the following:
<u>Required in the coming months:</u>

- Ride Cymbal + cymbal stand
- Crash Cymbal + cymbal stand. Diameters: 16" and 18" are most common
- Floor Tom (2 maximum). Diameters: 14" and 16" are the most common
- Rack Tom (1 or 2 is fine) + stand or mount. Diameters: 10" and 12" are most common (Use a 12" if only getting one)

<u>Extras:</u>

- Splash cymbal + mounted arm. Diameters: 8" or 10" are most common
- Cowbell + mount for kick drum
- China Cymbal + stand. Any diameter

With cymbals, try to avoid cheap brands/models. They make all the difference in the sound of a drumkit. As with any instrument, the student must be inspired to play it. That requires better quality. You do not need high-end gear, of course. For a new student who is buying a used kit, you will spend between $150 and $400 (U.S. dollars) for basics.

"*Can we go without a drumkit until s/he is ready*?"

Yes, you can. However, the student will only learn basic rudiments. For lessons that require a drumkit s/he can use the "knee and floor" method, emulating a drumkit on the knees and on the floor (kick drum). But this simulation will only work for so long, and s/he will become uninspired quickly. While each child is different, my advice is "*if you are going to do this, then do this.*" **Make the student feel like this is important and the student will most often own up to the challenge**.

"*Where can I look for a drumkit?*"

A reputable music store will have used kits. Tell them the basic components you need. Look for Internet deals on eBay or Amazon. Again, I advise *used* equipment at this stage.

Regardless of where you look, you should feel free to call your instructor with any questions. Know that your instructor will have an invested interest in his/her students obtaining a good quality, *inexpensive* drumkit.

"*I found this <off brand> kit new for real cheap!*"

My first instinct is plainly, **"no."** Anything from a department store shelf or that looks like a generic toy is going to sound like a generic toy, feel like a generic toy and be generally uninspiring. Find something used, and *real*. Bearing in mind that each brand has subsequent models and several variations of what is included, there are so many to choose from that it is mind-boggling. This is why I suggested starting *small*.

Still, any one of these brands is highly reputable (plus others – there are dozens more great brands):

- Ludwig
- Pearl
- DW
- Gretsch
- Premier
- Mapex
- Slingerland
- Sonor
- Tama
- Yamaha

For cymbals, you can choose any one of these brands:

- Zildjian
- Paiste
- Sabian
- Istanbul
- Meinl
- TRX
- Soultone
- Bosphorus

DRUMSET COMPONENTS

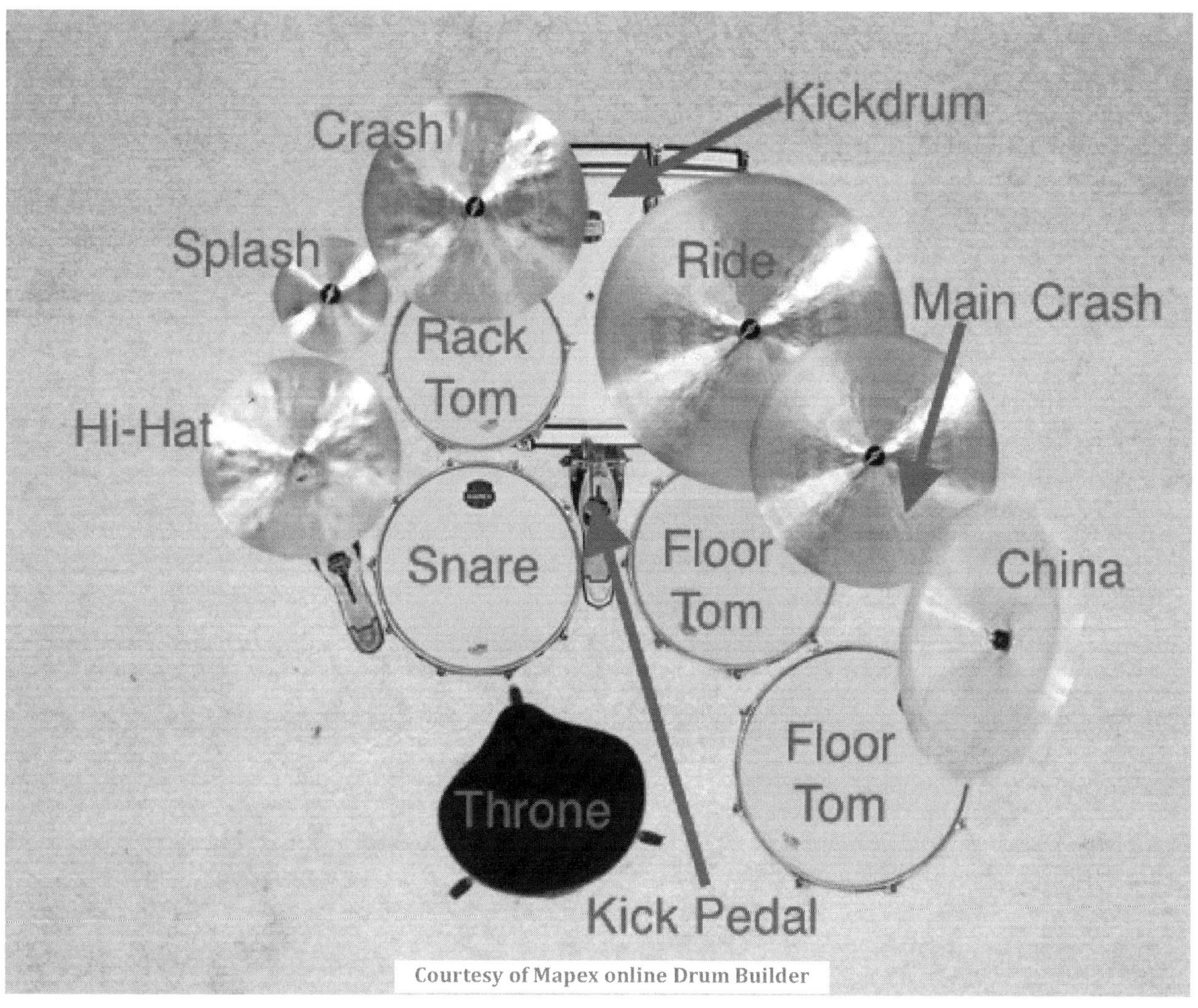

Courtesy of Mapex online Drum Builder

This configuration is called, "one up, two down," referring to the rack and floor toms. The ride cymbal in this photo is placed in the standard location, but there are no rules. Start with the kick, snare, hi-hat and ride. Add floor toms and rack tom next.

Student Assignment Sheet

Student Name: ____

Date: ______/______/__________

Rudiment(s): ____

Exercise(s): ____

Assignment(s): ____

Assignment(s): ____

Assignment(s): ____

Notes: ____

Song(s): ____

Date: ______/______/__________

Rudiment(s): ____

Exercise(s): ____

Assignment(s): ____

Assignment(s): ____

Assignment(s): ____

Notes: ____

Song(s): ____

Date: ______/______/__________

Rudiment(s): ____

Exercise(s): ____

Assignment(s): ____

Assignment(s): ____

Assignment(s): ____

Notes: ____

Song(s): ____

I) How To Read Dotted Notes

Whereas one quarter note occupies two eight notes:

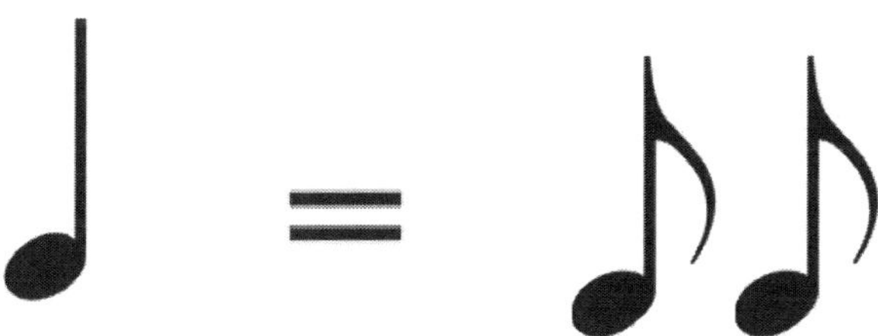

A *dotted* quarter note occupies three eight notes:

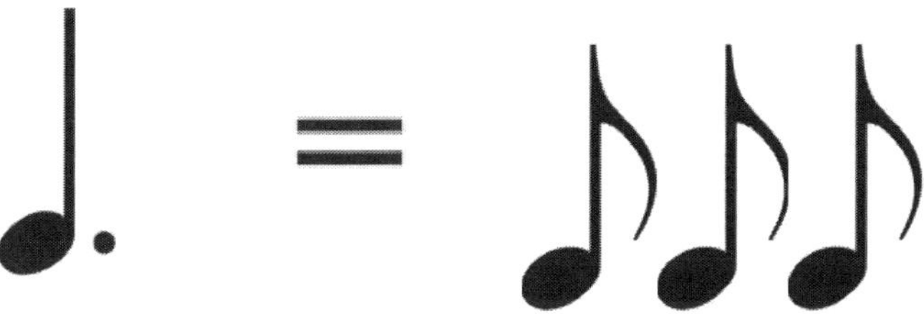

Whereas one eight note occupies two sixteenth notes:

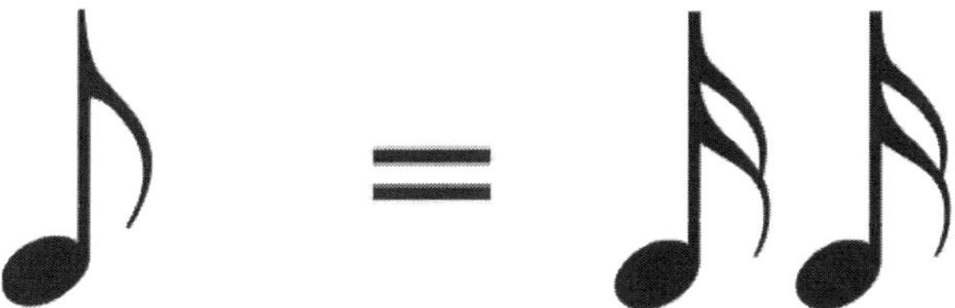

A *dotted* eight note occupies three sixteenth notes:

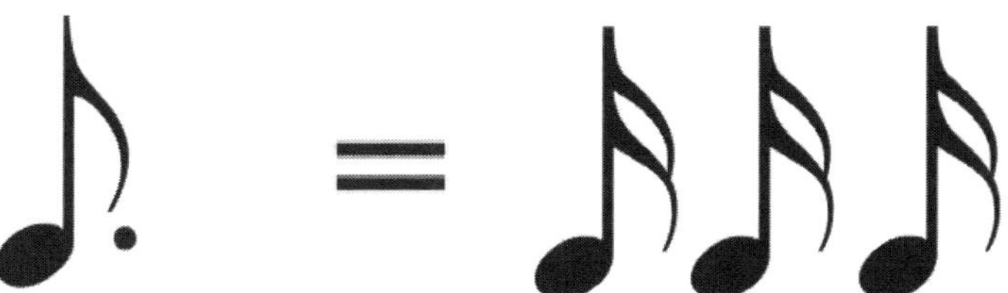

J) The Proper Care and Feeding of Your Drumkit

Caring for a drumset appears to be a lost art. I always hope to impart some sensible and reasonable drumkit care lessons to all of my students. Often, a student will bring his/her drums to me as their one-hour lesson on how to tune a kit, which I am going to discuss here. But there is so much more to taking care of this instrument. I've said before that the drums are unlike any instrument on the planet. It's very true. It has its own stigma attached to it. There is an entire world of drumming out there all of its own. There are entire stores dedicated to just drums. It uses all four limbs. It breaks down in various different ways. Things fall apart nearly each performance or practice. It can be highly aerobic and athletic. And maintenance of a drumkit is no less abnormal.

Tuning

I have been asked many times, as have most instructors, "What is the best way to tune drums." You'll get as many answers as there are instructors to answer the question. All I can do is offer you the exact science behind what I do, as I was instructed at the Atlanta Institute of Music by Tom Knight. It's not mystical or ambiguous. It's deliberate and purposeful. If there were nothing else I did to ensure I had a good sound, it would be to tune my drums exactly the same way, exactly *this way*, each and every time. Why this way? Because I like how it sounds. It is *my sound.* That's the only reason I, or any drummer, should require. If this way doesn't work for you, try a lower tuning set, a higher tuning set, and see what works. If it still doesn't sound right to you, change the snare tuning, and only the snare tuning. Sometimes the snare tuning makes the whole kit sound different. If it still doesn't work then this tuning method is simply not for you. But I can tell you that it works on every drumset exactly the same way, with the same results, each time.

First – abandon all forms of muting the drumhead. Just get rid of them. You will want a nice long sustained tone out of your drums.
Second – My preference is single-ply heads. Sometimes double-ply heads work, but they don't sustain as long. Of course, this is preference issue. In either case, do not use *old drumheads*.
Third – Get a tuner. Usually you can download one for a smart phone or iPod touch.

I have various different schemes depending upon the band and the venue (a place at a band or artist performs). This is the one I most commonly use:

Drum	Top/Batter	Bottom/Resonant
16	E2	A2
14	A2	D3
12	D3	G3
10	G3	C4
8	C4	F4
Snare	E4	A4
Kick:	A	A

This tuning scheme has each batter/top drumhead tuned to a *perfect fourth* (five ½ steps) lower than the resonant/bottom drumhead. This only works with the even-sized toms. Odd-sized toms (13, 15) will not work within the above tuning scheme. If you have an odd tom, improvise. But the method is to tune the *batter drumhead of the lowest tom first* (16" in this case), then the resonant drumhead, which will be five ½ steps higher. Notice it matches the batter drumhead of the 14" tom? That's to allow both drumheads to resonate together in the same pitch. Use this pattern all the way up to an 8" tom. I have had no luck using this scheme on a 6" tom. But it will work great on an 18" floor tom!

Each drum must be dismounted from their stands or rack. Place each drum on a soft surface to mute one drumhead while tuning the other. It will sound strange this way. But when both drumheads are tuned (after you've flipped it over and tuned the other side) it will sound glorious. A cool way to tune your floor toms without so many struggles is to place it atop the seat of your throne. The legs will just dangle while the resonant drumhead is muted.

The kick drum is its own lesson. But the short of it is, use your ear. The kick and the snare are the heart and pulse of any drumkit. If they don't sound to your liking, you will not enjoy playing. Above all, use your ear when tuning. But this will give you a dependable method.

Maintenance

Things fall apart. After every performance there is always something I have to fix. The drums often fall apart, requiring immediate repair, *during* performances. You will need to learn how to manage that on your own. But afterward, when you have the time try a couple of things to keep your kit running smoothly.

1. Check all screws and springs on your kick drum pedal.
2. Check for missing cymbal-stand sleeves that protect your cymbal.
3. Take the drumheads off. Remove all the debris. Never put anything oily on them.
4. While you have the drumheads off, tighten all the screws, including the air hole.
5. Check your snare wires. If they are snapping off, replace them.
6. Put some oil (I use CLP gun cleaner, actually) in each lug where the tension rods go. Too much will cause them to slip a lot during performances so go easy.
7. Clean your cymbals (see below).
8. Scrub away any rust spots on the drum hoops and hardware.
9. Dust them. In time, dust will destroy the finish of your drums.

Repairs

You can do it yourself. Don't be afraid. If something broke, just fix it. I cannot tell you how many times I've fixed something. I've had the chain of a hi-hat snap at the pedal. I fixed it. I've reused broken cymbals by either drilling holes in them for a cool FX cymbal or stacking them for an X-hat. I've rebuilt an entire gong bass because the bearing edge (where the drumhead sits) was destroyed. I've swapped hi-hat parts and changed them from three-legged to two-legged stands. I've stripped away drum wraps and stained the drum the color I wanted. I've used spare parts from twenty years ago to create another drum. Just keep everything and don't be intimidated. There are no "drum repair" shops that I've ever seen. It's a community. Ask people. Hit the search engines on the Internet.

Drumheads

If your snare drumhead is worn in the middle, you need to replace it. If it is coated but has lost its grit and roughness, you need to replace it. If you removed any drumhead and there are ripples in it, replace it. If you've had it for more than a year and play regularly, replace it. If you are struggling to get a good sound from it no matter what you do, replace it. Generally, I replace mine about once every 12-18 months because I do not *pound* my drums. The kick drumhead could last you years if you don't pound a hole in it. Use something to protect the kick drumhead from the beater. The cost is negligible. But the kick drumhead is about $2 per inch, which is about twice the cost of all others. You don't need a pillow in your kick drum, but if you do use one make sure it is free floating so you can use it only when you need it. I keep a rug laced at the bottom of my kick below the pillow to absorb the hollow sounding high-ends.

General Protection

Don't let two drums bang together while playing them. That causes ruts and cuts and scrapes. If you must have them together, put a towel in between the drums where they clank together. Keep the hi-hat cymbals from touching anything around them. Prevent hoops from clanking into each other. Ensure that your crash cymbals have plenty of room to wobble without hitting anything else. Otherwise they will invariably crack. Ensure your cymbals are not cranked too tightly. Cranking them too tight not only dilutes their natural sustain and sound but will also cause them to crack and die an unnatural death!

Always use drum and cymbal bags. Soft bags are fine as long as they are padded well. They are worth the investment if you plan on carrying your stuff around more than a couple times a year. When they transport, damage occurs, without fail. If you have no bags, use as many towels and blankets as you can! Always protect them!

Cymbal Cleaning

If there's one thing we drummers do not look forward to, it's cleaning cymbals. But if you'll follow this procedure, it will much smoother for you.
What you will need:

1. A good cymbal polisher
2. Liquid soap of any kind
3. A *scrub-free* spray cleaner (such as for the shower).

First – apply the polisher with your fingers. It will get very messy. Avoid the logos on the cymbal. Sometimes it will remove them. Scrub in circles until it turns black. This is the oxidation being removed. This oxidation will cause your cymbal to gradually lose its luster and the brilliance in its sound. Do this to both sides.

Second – Head to the shower or the outside faucet and wash it off. Now … it just looks terrible. So, this is where you add a little soap to it in the running water. Scrub the soap all around until as much of the oxidation is removed as possible.

Third – Spray the scrub-free shower cleaner on and (with clean hands!) scrub away the last of the polish and oxidation. Check it in various lighting to ensure you've removed all the streaks. Your cymbal should now be restored to its former brilliance.

K) DRUMKIT ERGONOMICS

The importance of getting your drumkit setup comfortably cannot be overstated. If you are overreaching you'll get shoulder fatigue. If you lack room to reach properly, you'll cramp or whack a knuckle. If your hips are below your knees you'll lack power in your delivery. If the cymbals are not within the proper distance, you'll either struggle to reach them for a 'choke' or bleed on them with your fingers.

Just as important as all this, if you don't set up your drums to work with your body dimensions (which will continually change especially under the age of 25), you will not be comfortable and not play well. Amongst the chief of these items is where your throne is positioned relative to your feet. Looking from an upright position on your throne, you should not be able to see your ankles, and your toes should be just in front of your knees. Your waistline should be at least slightly above your knees. Most of all, **you should be comfortable**. Put your feel flat on the ground – no pedals – and look at them. Naturally, they fell where they should go. There are always compromises to make, but this is basically where your pedals should go.

When you strike the snare your left hand (in matched grip) should not struggle to avoid your knees. Keep that in mind when you set your throne height. The snare hoop should be about waist/buckle high, give or take, depending upon your body dimensions.

The hi-hat is next. Close your eyes before you place the hi-hat stand. Have someone hold it out of reach. Now play your hi-hat comfortably as if it is there. Open your eyes. That's were it should go. Have someone move it there. That same process is how you will arrange your ride, crash cymbals, toms and floor toms. Have someone hold them out of reach. Play where it is comfortable. Don't concern yourself with looks. Ergonomics are about comfort and playability, not visuals and having an impressive arrangement. Regardless of how many pieces you have, there will always be compromises. And there is no "right way" to do it. These concepts apply to every drummer, regardless of dimensions or whether you play right- or left-handed.

Photo: Courtesy of Katie Lynn Moss Photography

Section II:
Reference Materials

A) Reading Drum Music

B) Triplet Combination Patterns

Rudiments

♩ = 90
r r l l
Double-stroke
f
R l l r
Double-stroke inverted
R l l r r L
Swiss Six
R l l r r L
6-Stroke Roll
R llrr L
6-Stroke
R l r L r l
Single-stroke triplet
r r r l l l
Triple Stroke
R l l r l l
Drag Triplet
r r l l r r l l r r l l
Dbl-Stroke Triplet
R l l r r l L r r l l r
Inverted dbl-stroke triplet
r r l l R l l r r L
5-Stroke
rrll R llrr L
5-Stroke
r r l l r r L l l r r l l R
7-Stroke
r r l l r r L
7-stroke triplet
rrllrr L llrrll R
7-Stroke
r r l l r r l l R
9-Stroke
rrllrrll R
9-Stroke
r r l l r r l l R
9-Stroke Triplet
r r l l r r l l R L
10-Stroke
rrllrrll R L
10-Stroke

Rudiments
R l r r L r l l
Paradiddle - (straight)
R l l r L r r l
Paradiddle - (inverted)
R r l r L l r l
Paradiddle - (reversed)
R l r l L r l r
Paradiddle - (inverted dbl)
R l r l r r L r l r l l
Double Paradidle - (straight)
R l l r l r L r r l r l
Double Paradidle - (inverted)
R r L l
Double Paradidle - (reversed)
R l L r
Double Paradidle - (inverted dbl)
3
l R r L
Flam
r L R L
Flam Accent
l R R L
Swiss Army Triplet
l R L r L R
Inverted Flam Tap
l R R r L l
Flam Tap
l R L R R r L R L L
Flam Paradiddle
l R R l r r L L R L
Single Flammed Mill
l R L R L l R
Flamacue
l R L R r L
Pataflafla
r r L l l R
Drag
l R l l R r L r r L
Flam Drag
l l R L r r L R
Single Drag Tap
l l R l l R L
Double Drag Tap

2/3

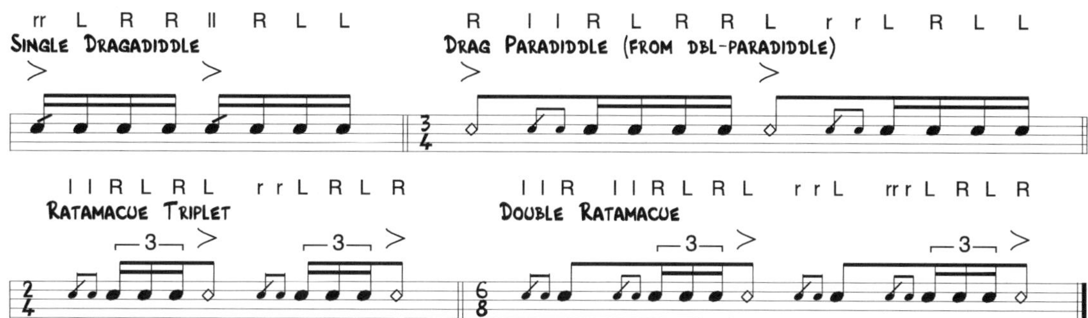
Rudiments
rr L R R ll R L L
Single Dragadiddle
R l l R L R R L r r L R L L
Drag Paradiddle (from dbl-paradiddle)
l l R L R L r r L R L R
Ratamacue Triplet
l l R l l R L R L r r L rrr L R L R
Double Ratamacue

3/3

December 19, 2015 – Lefty Williams Band, Dunedin Brewery, Dunedin, FL

Section III: Exercises

A) Exercise #1: Mirroring The Hands

During the beginner stage of drumming it is normal and expected to have a weaker hand or foot that doesn't perform as well as the other. The most obvious solution is to spend hours upon days upon weeks in rote repetition to resolve the issue. But this can become horribly boring. The main issue is that the weaker limb has nothing to measure against without a *mirrored* comparison with the stronger limb. This requires supreme attention to detail. It could be the way the hand (or foot) is positioned relative to the wrist (or ankle). The fingers or thumb could be in the wrong position; it could be a centimeter difference in where how the hand is turned or which fingers are being used correctly, or any myriad of issues. The best solution is a visual comparison: Mirroring the hands.

The student must hold the sticks in matched grip and perform the task with the stronger hand, then with the weaker hand. One by one, nearly each difference will be more quickly identified and resolved. Also, it is very important to remember, during any exercise that requires striking a drum or practice pad, the stick should be at about a 30 degree angle. The height is a big indicator. *If the sticks or pedal beaters are not reaching the same angle, then something is wrong.* Look at the differences in thumb positions. Look at which fingers are doing the most work. Which knuckles are bending? Are the wrists behaving identical to each other? Little nuances make all the difference.

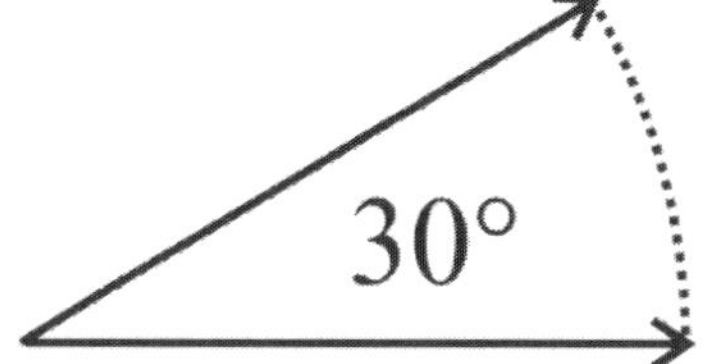

B) Exercise #2: Forearm Slap

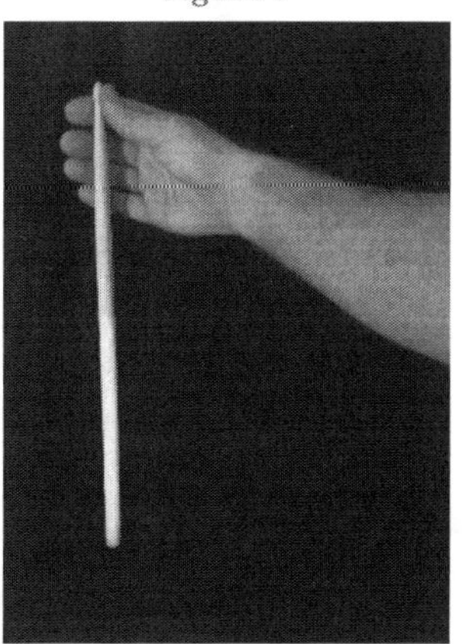
Figure 7

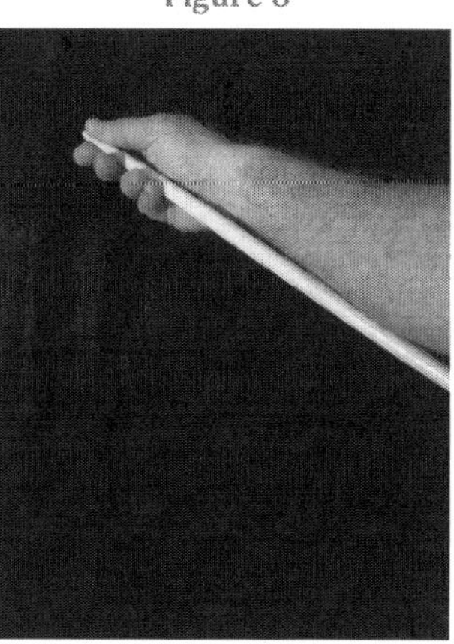
Figure 8

This exercise strengthens the motion of the fingers for a matched grip strike. Sometimes students overthink this motion to the point of becoming comatose. To simplify the idea, I will often get the student to act as if they are throwing the stick, and then ask them to analyze the motion. It's natural. There's really no thinking involved and throwing the stick produces the same arm and joint motions required for striking a drum! Though teaching how the fingers operate in the hand during a strike seems to get more complicated. I developed this exercise for the students to work on anywhere, any time.

The stick should remain in a 45-degree angle from the arm, which will be held outward as such (figure 7): Pull the stick inward using only the fingers (figure 8). Do not flex the wrist. This is a finger-only exercise. **It is designed to strengthen the fingers** for the French grip. Repeat multiple times. You will eventually feel the 'burn' in the forearm. Keep this up until you gain speed. Don't start fast. Go for good technique. The speed will come.

C) Exercise #3: Wrist Trapping

The purpose of this exercise is to teach the fingers to move independently. No two students are going to be wired the same. Some students have a difficult time initially moving the fingers independently from the wrist muscles. *Wrist trapping* will train wrist and finger muscles to work independently from one another. A student with past musical experience on guitar or piano will likely bring some built-in dexterity into drumming. Since every student has different needs, this exercise may or may not be required.

To perform this exercise, simply grab above and below the wrist and lock it using the other hand (figures 9 & 10):

Figure 9 Figure 10

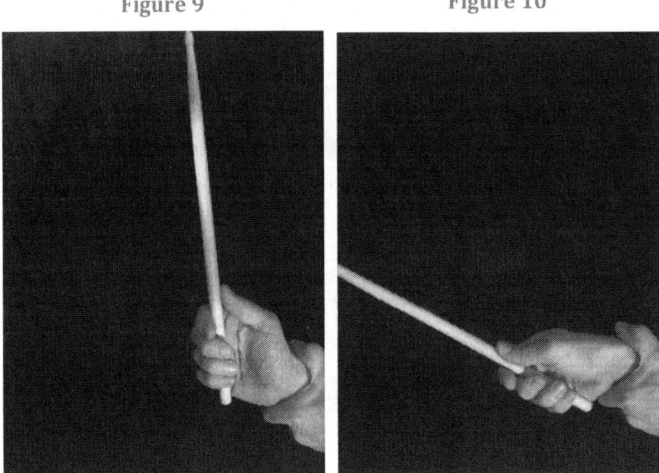

D) Exercise #4: Leg Pressure

One of the more difficult hills to climb as a new student is learning to use the calve muscles instead of the **hip flexors**. The hip flexors (figure 11) are the muscles that connect the top of your thigh to your hip. Hip flexor usage is debilitating to a performance. As well, it causes imbalance, sluggishness, a lack of dynamics and inaccuracy on the hip and, eventually, hip flexor strain. More over, it is entirely unnecessary. Using this muscle to lift the leg is called the *stomp method*. It is generally how students get started, especially younger students who have not quite strengthened his or her calve muscles yet. It is a very bad habit, and usually difficult to break.

Figure 11

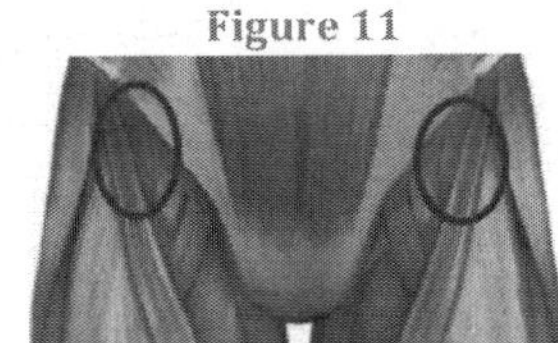

Image source: http://www.sports-injury-info.com/image-files/hip-pain-hip-flexor.jpg

The best way I have found for students to learn to drop this bad habit, regardless of age or drumming experience, is to **apply full-body weight over the knee** (with the foot on the pedal) using both hands, leaning forward, applying full pressure to the leg. **This forces the leg to abandon the hip flexor muscles** and use calve muscles instead. For explanation on calve muscles techniques please re-read Section I-(b)&(c) of this book on *Technique, Stick Grip and Pedal Control.*

With full body pressure on the knee, and the *beater buried into the head*, push upward using the calve muscle. This resistance training should continue for **at least a week** on and off and can be done anywhere. While the foot is on the pedal and raised using the calve muscle, drop the heel. Simply release the resisting pressure by relaxing the muscle, and land firmly on the *ball of the foot*, not the heel.

The heel should be about half an inch above the ground. This should cause impact of the beater onto the kick drumhead.

E) Exercise #5: Bouncing Stick Drop

Initially learning to allow the sticks to *do the work for you* is one of the most difficult lessons to surmount, especially for young, new students. It is somewhat counter-intuitive to NOT try and force the strike. However, the natural kinetics that occur from the combination of the drumhead tension and proper use of the stick are what make drumming physically easy. If you or any of your students are not experiencing this physical ease within drumming then the stick technique should be re-evaluated. There should be little to no tension in the hands, wrists, fingers and certainly none whatsoever in the arms and shoulders under any circumstances.

The most effective and simplest (albeit, painfully tedious) way that I have found to teach this relaxation for double-stroke rolls is to simply allow the sticks to bounce freely on a neoprene drum pad (keeping the thumb *on* the stick at all times). The higher the tip of the stick, the greater the rebound and longer it will bounce. This *will* reorient the brain into permitting the stick to bounce. It will teach the student that it is okay to *let go* and let the stick rebound. Double-stroke rolls *are not individually struck.* **A double-stroke roll is** NOT **played with two hits on each stick.** Rather, it is one strike plus one bounce. The brain naturally wants to force each of these hits. It is up to the instructor to teach the student to let go and to allow the sticks to bounce/rebound.

In my experience, this is the most effective way of teaching double-stroke rolls:

1) Allow the sticks to bounce freely using French grip. Just drop the tip of the stick onto the pad and allow a multiple bounce strike. If necessary, turn the hands upside down (palm up) and release the sticks during this bounce to teach the hands what it feels like. Practice this for one entire week as often as is possible. Get accustomed to the way this feels in the hands;
2) Begin "catching" the stick after two hits (one strike = two hits). The fingers will release the stick as it drops, and curl around the stick as it is caught (loosely, of course). Work with this for an entire week at least, an hour at a time. Turn on a movie to prevent boredom;
3) Next, bounce the right stick only, then catch it; bounce the left stick only, catch; repeat. This will create a good foundation for the double-stroke roll. After some time they can be combined into a slow double-stroke using high stick height and even hits.

F) Exercise #6: Open-Close Palm Coordination

The intent of this exercise is to create the necessary coordination required for the drop-catch method mentioned in Exercise #5, but is ordinarily not required until the intermediate stage where it becomes more useful for speeding up rhythm "#-e-&" or "#-&-a" patterns. It is also used in beginner stages for the shuffle "a-#" if the student is ready or hungry for that level of learning. Warning: the drop-catch method is not a quickly learned technique. It could take an hour a night for upwards of a month (approximately 30 hours) before it becomes natural, depending upon the student. The real challenge on the drumkit is relearning to coordinate the rest of the body with this technique. Learning to open or close during a strike with the opposite hand, or with the feet, is an involved process.

1. Place the pad of the thumb against the middle knuckle of the third finger (figure 12), palms facing upward. This is the fulcrum in which the sticks will move.

Figure 12

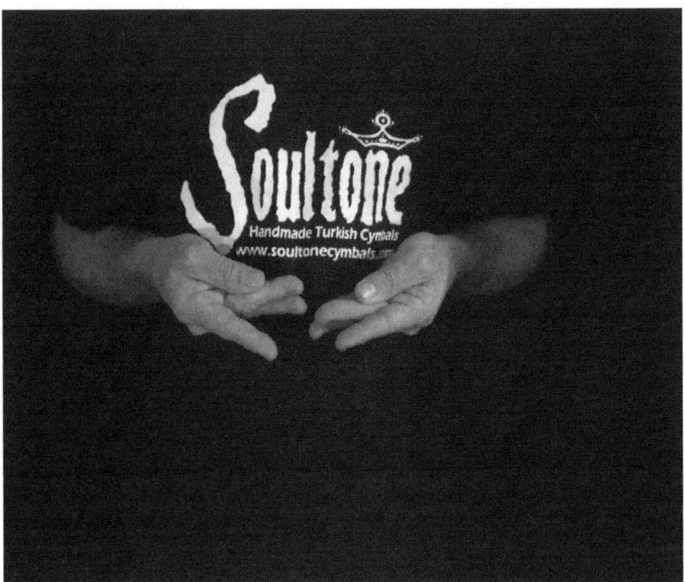

2. Close both hands, keeping the pad of the thumb against the middle knuckle (figure 13).

Figure 13

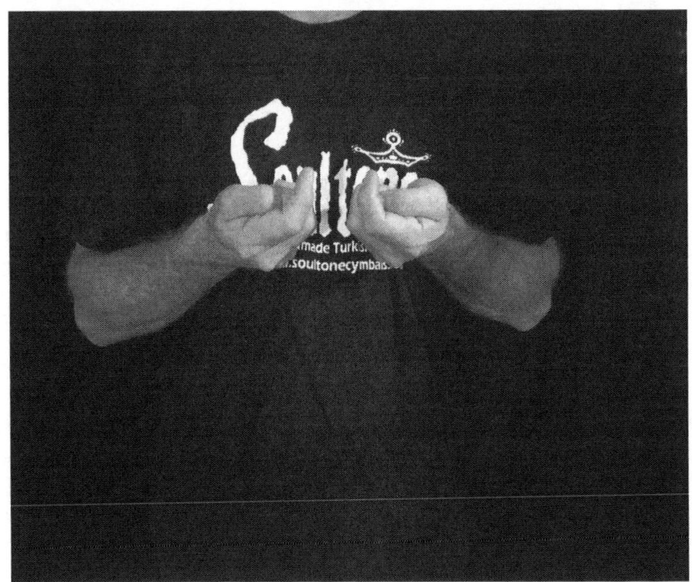

3. Keeping the thumb in the same location, simultaneously bring the right hand down, face the palm downward and open the fingers (figure 14),

Figure 14

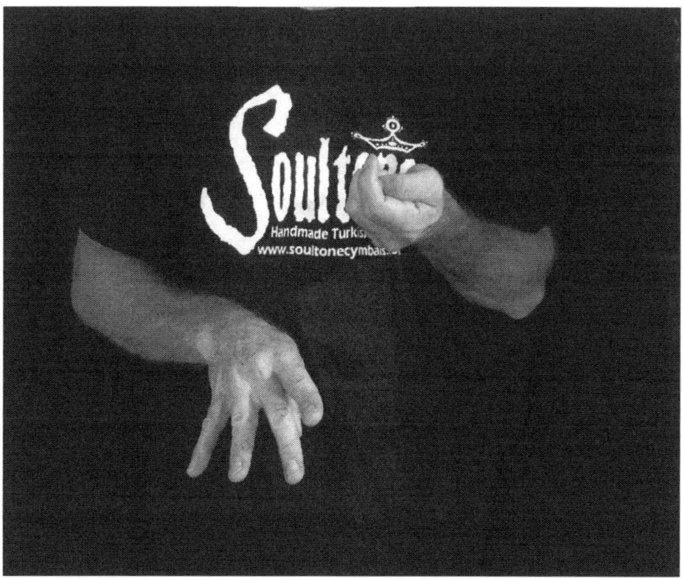

4. then reverse them (figure 15). This will be more difficult at first than you might think.

Figure 15

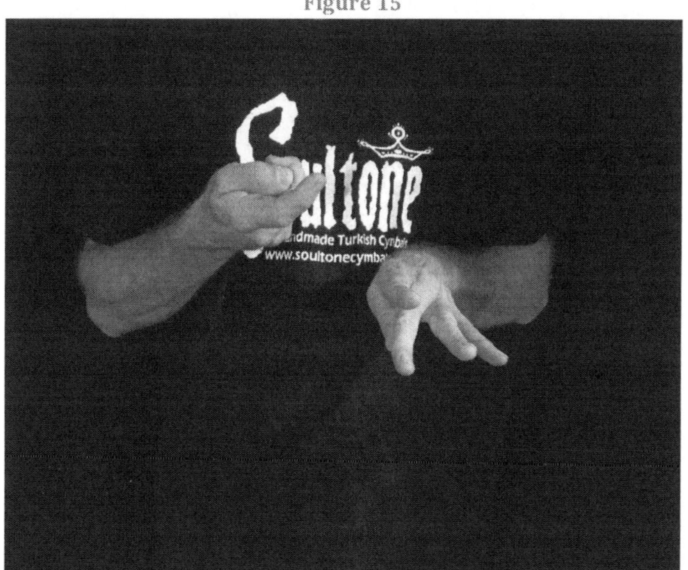

5. Lastly, bring both hands down, facing palm down, fingers opened (figure 16).

Figure 16

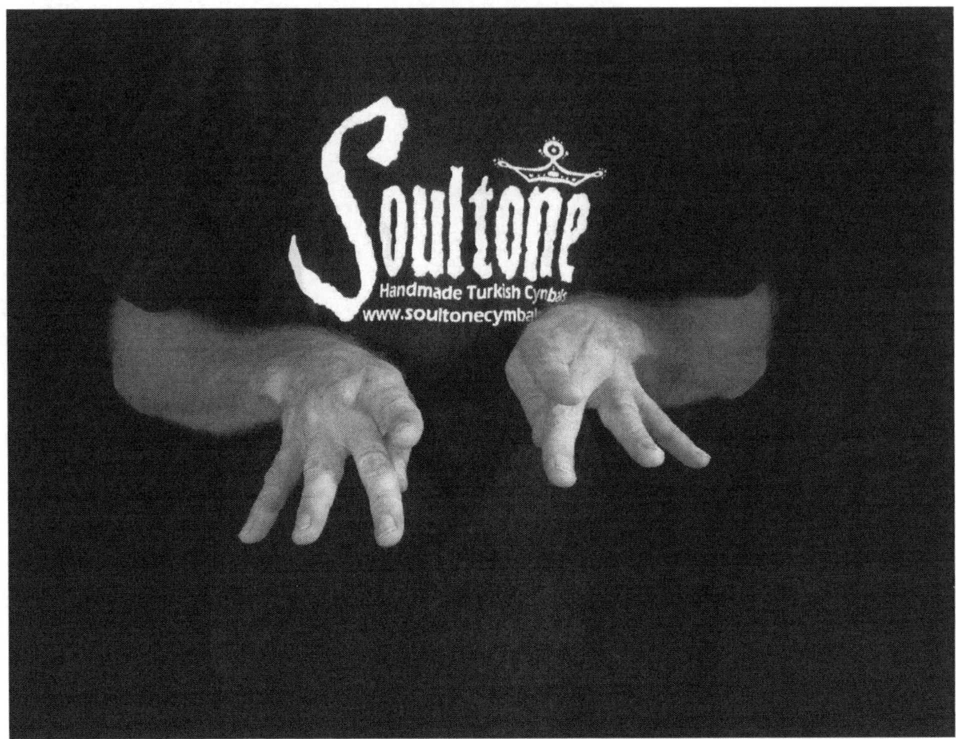

6. Now, adding sticks to your hands, keeping the same "pinch" of the thumb and third finger, repeat the previous steps (figures 17-21):

Figure 17

Figure 18

Figure 19

Figure 20

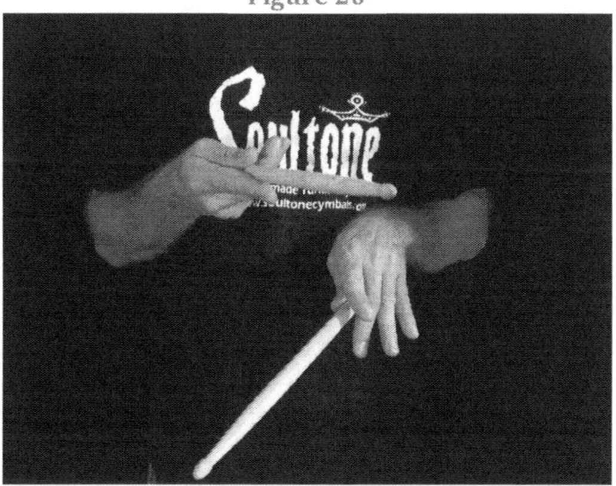

You should only need to perform this exercise initially. It should not be required as a repeating exercise.

Figure 21

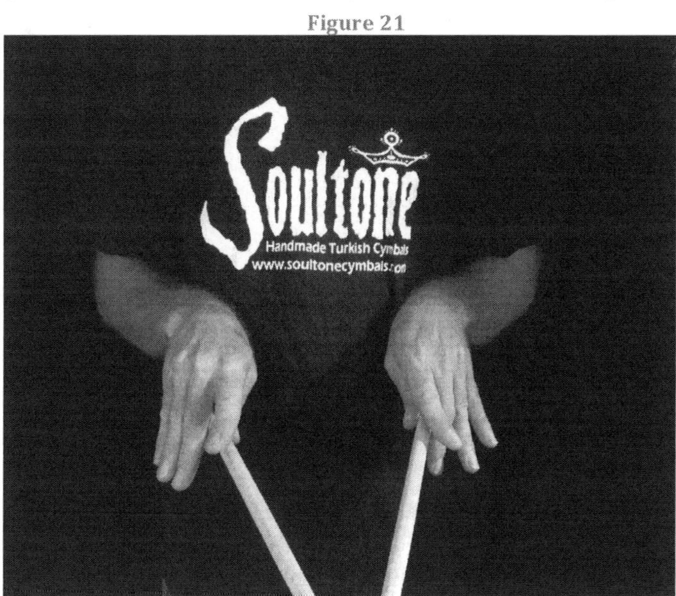

G) Exercise #7: Foot heel-toe tapping

At times the student will find him- or herself unable to perform combinations of foot techniques such as heel-only on right foot and ankle-only on left foot, or to rock the left foot while the right uses a more constant technique. It is important in building a good repertoire of skills (which in turn allows more freedom of expression on the instrument), to be able to combine any foot technique at any given time, with confidence.

The following simple, yet frustrating, exercise will quickly provide the necessary coordination to be able to combine any of the foot techniques together. No illustrations required:

1) Sit with both feet flat on the ground;
2) lift your right toe, rocking back on the heel;
3) lift the left heel, rocking forward on the ball of the foot;
4) reverse, repeat until it is comfortable.

Next, experiment by rocking one foot back and forth while tapping the other with the toe, or with the heel. You can do triplets with one foot: forward, forward, back or back, back forward. Or, doubles: FFBB, BBFF, all while doing something completely different with the other foot. This exercise will truly be as much fun as it is exasperating.

After a couple tries, you should never really need to do this exercise again for basic drumming. If you desire a more advanced drumming approach, keep experimenting with it until you master half a dozen or so combinations. And remember: in all things creative, only your level of desire fashions your limits!

October 5, 2013 – JC Bridwell – Under the oaks music fest, Cleveland, GA

Section IV: Curriculum

Level One:
Beginner (No Belt)
Basics

1.1 - All Possible 8th and 16th Note Rhythms

Beginner Reading – Written Drum Music

Learning the first page of drum material in this book requires *zero prior reading or playing experience.* The student will decisively learn how to read (at a primary level) within a guaranteed five minutes if the instructor will teach as prescribed in Section 1(e) *Steps to Learning Any Rhythm.*

Starting at the Beginning

What better place to begin, right? First, right foot goes on the kick drum pedal, left foot on the hi-hat pedal, left stick on the snare, right stick *crossed over the left* on the hi-hat cymbals. If you are left-handed, go ahead and feel free to learn open-handed drumming with right hand on snare, left hand on hi-hat. This also allows more freedom to move around the kit. Advanced right-handed players play this way at times. I have found it to be rather liberating. Whichever you choose, *stay with it.*

Page Instructions

For the student to learn to read this page with no prior experience, the instructor simply points to each *beat* (with any number of notes), asking the student to **play only that beat**. So for beat one on this page, the student plays the hi-hat and the kick … just that and only that … saying aloud, "*one*" – then repeat for the next beat, saying, "*and.*" Continue this method and the intimidation factor will simply vanish as the student finds him- or herself reading and playing for the first time. Play it a-rhythmically. That is, **do not try to play it in rhythm** just yet. Get the coordination down first. There is absolutely no need to understand beat-value (beat-occupation) at this point. That will come in time, with the proper amount of practice and counting these exercises.

This is called "*All Possible Eight and Sixteenth Note Rhythms*" because there truly are no other possible *fundamental* rhythms. This page is based on the 16th notes listed in "*1.5 - All 16th Note Beats.*" Learning each of these will develop the necessary coordination to play nearly anything (on the kick drum) by combining each of them any way you wish. But that will come later in the curriculum. Be patient for now.

I have split the page up into two major parts: 8th notes and 16th notes. The smaller sections are based on how many kick drum notes are *played together*. So, one-, two- and three-note patterns are different sections within each part. This categorization is used throughout this book. As mentioned in the next page, 1.2, there are approximately 33 of these rhythms, depending upon how you quantify it. Twenty-three of them are on this page. Twelve are triplet rhythms.

I have deliberately *not* written the rhythm counts (#,e,&,a) above each rhythm. I feel that would be a distraction and would become a crutch for the new student learning to read. The objective of counting is to be able to relieve the student of the sheet music altogether and to *internalize* the rhythm as much as memorize it. If the count was written above each beat then I would be enabling the student to use a crutch. But feel free, if it helps, to write a few more as needed above each rhythm.

Use rimshots on each of the snare hits. Try to hit the exact center of the snare. A rimshot is a strike in the center of the snare **and** the rim of the metal snare hoop. It will create 'pop' or 'crack' sound because it is utilizing the actual wood or metal shell. Get used to this idea. You will use it in every single page to follow.

Weekly Assignment week #1

- **Exercises:** The student's first one-week assignment is sections "*A & B*" *only.* It is of the utmost importance to **count, aloud, everything** played on this page. This will develop a sense of understanding of how beats work.

Weekly Assignment week #2

- **Exercises:** Section C and All 8ths. The student's next assignments will likely last more than one week, but that is entirely dependent upon how apt s/he is. I've had students breeze through the entire page in one week, and some take upwards of five weeks.

Weekly Assignment week #3 (2 weeks)

- **Exercises**: Section D, E, & F and All 16th notes. Learning to count in 16th notes has generally been a bit more difficult. I've explained it every way conceivable to every level and type of student and everyone gets it differently. But once you have it, you have it. Understand that this is math. Count each as written on the page. Remember, just because a count or beat is not present, it is not *missing* – it is a rest instead. That means that you cannot skip it because it is merely *silent*. So, count it without playing it. That is to say, count "#,e,&,a" all on each measure and only play the ones that are written like "1,-,&,a." Notice the silent "-" where the "e" should be. Count everything and only play what is written.

  Count
  Count
  Count
  Count
  Count

It can't be emphasized enough. Count, count, count, count … and count *aloud*. Don't be shy. Be loud.

1.1 - All Possible 8th and 16th Note Rhythms

♩ = 50

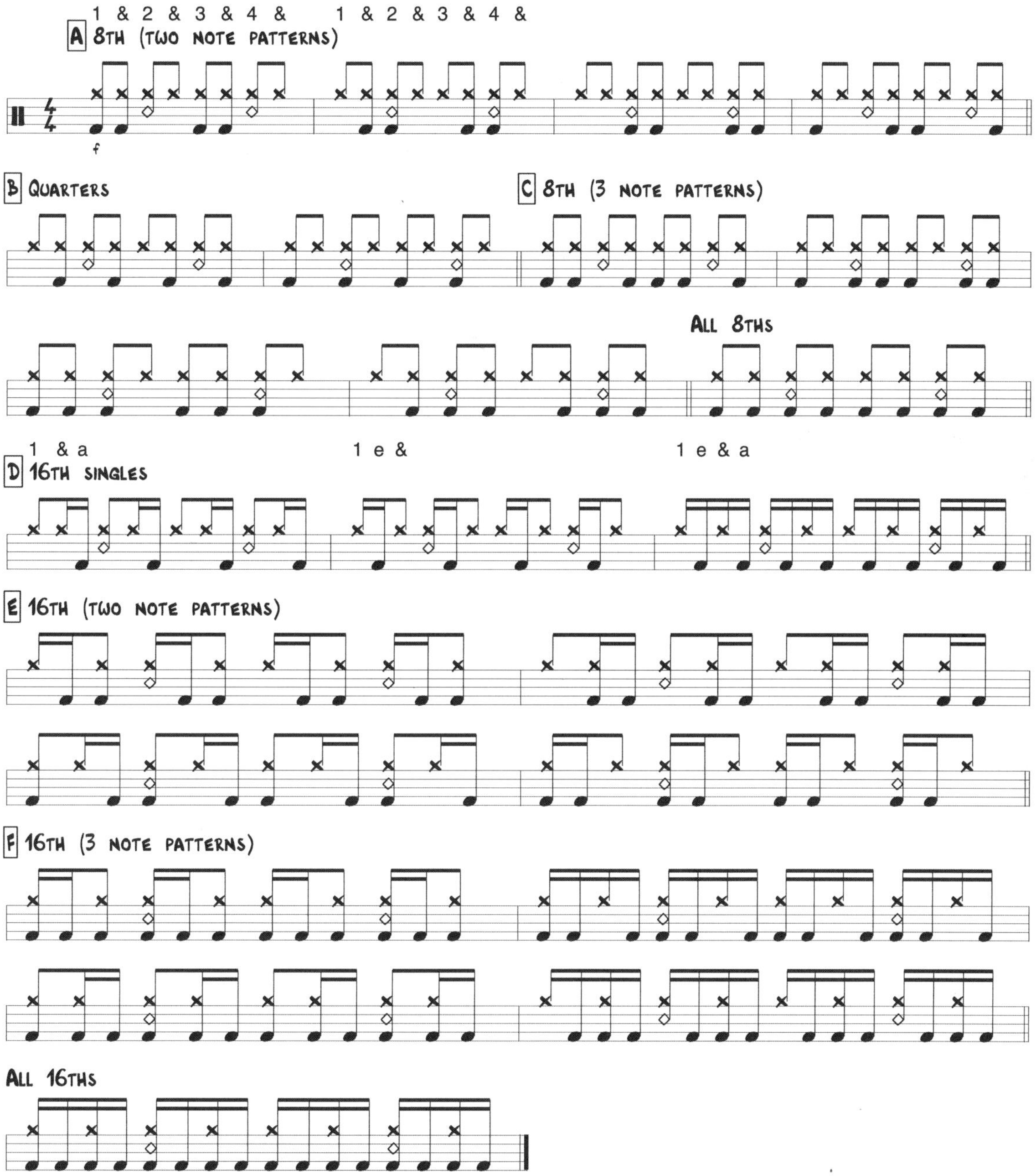

1 & 2 & 3 & 4 & 1 & 2 & 3 & 4 &

A 8TH (TWO NOTE PATTERNS)

f

B QUARTERS

C 8TH (3 NOTE PATTERNS)

ALL 8THS

1 & a 1 e & 1 e & a

D 16TH SINGLES

E 16TH (TWO NOTE PATTERNS)

F 16TH (3 NOTE PATTERNS)

ALL 16THS

1.2 - All 8th Note Triplet Beats

Page Instructions

There is, I'm certain, a mathematical limitation to exactly how many rhythms can be created. And if I were a statistician or mathematician I would hand that figure to you! But from my view, using just one hand/stick or just one foot/pedal (each is called a "voice"), there is a finite reality of rhythm constructs that can be used: about 33, depending upon how you quantify a pattern. For triplets, there are twelve.

As you progress in your coordination, you will want return to these concepts and create more complex combinations. I still do! First, begin by learning the basic rhythms on the next page using the kick drum. I often have the new student practice them first on kick drum, then learn the same notes/beats on snare, then combine them.

In this example, the first two measures are basic kick drum double-note patterns:

Figure 22

After learning the first two measures in figure 22, play the other two measures on the snare drum and the kick drum, as illustrated. The combination possibilities increase dramatically when you add the other foot/pedal and hand/stick over top of these rhythms like so:

Figure 23

Figure 23: The first row uses the hi-hat foot and kick drum foot; the second row uses the right hand and kick drum foot; the third row uses a combination of three voices. The student will likely never need to know all possible combinations. The intent is to build coordination. And it is entirely up to your imagination which pedal and stick combination you use.

Weekly Assignment

* **Exercise:** Combine at least four measures using kick and snare. Create your own! Make it difficult!

1.2 - All Possible 8th Note Triplet Beats

♩ = 68

1 e a 2 e a 3 e a 4 e a

SINGLE-BEAT PATTERNS

DOUBLE-BEAT PATTERNS

ALTERNATING-BEAT PATTERNS

TRIPLE-BEAT PATTERN

/00/

QUADRUPLE-BEAT PATTERN

ALL

1.3 - All 8th Note Triplet Rhythms

Page Instructions

As in the last exercise, these twelve measures are the basic rhythmic constructs upon which all 8th note triplet rhythms are created. These are the bedrock foundational skillsets for the beginner student. This exercise contains rhythms that are used in many ballads, blues, rock and country songs.

A beginner or intermediate student will not likely use the Triple-Kick drum and Quadruple-Kick drum Patterns. But these exercises will help to build coordination. Learn those two measures once and then move on. The others are more important and the skills learned here will be used in the coming lessons.

Again: count, count, count, count. When the student learns them well enough to kick off the crutch, s/he can stop counting. The intent is to find the weak areas and drill into them until they are stronger, not to depend upon the written material. The student should have the expectation of eventually performing these rhythms with eyes shut.

And just as a matter of education, note that the Triple-Kick drum Pattern is based on quads, and the Quadruple-Kick drum Pattern is based on quints – if you add the rest note together with them.

Weekly Assignment

- **Exercise:** Learn each part of 1.3 (*All Possible 8th Note Triple Rhythms*) as written, only thru line three. Count through any parts that give you trouble. Remember that counting should be used to assist you in your learning. Look away from the material whenever you can. Do not worry about the triple and quadruple kick patterns at this time.

- Rudiment: The Single-Stroke roll (figure 24) is the foundation of all drumming. You must be able to perform a single-stroke roll to play almost anything beyond a basic beat. A single-stroke roll is played: R-L-R-L repeatedly. The way you will begin to learn this basic rudiment is by playing the following:

Figure 24

Practice this at the fastest pace you can without error. If you make a mistake, you're practicing too fast. Remember to use the proper grip and as little arm movement as possible. Repeat it over and over on your practice pad (or the floor, or bed or pillow). It should be a smooth motion. Use a mirror if you have one to see what your arms, wrists and hands are doing.

1.3 - All Possible 8th Note Triplet Rhythms

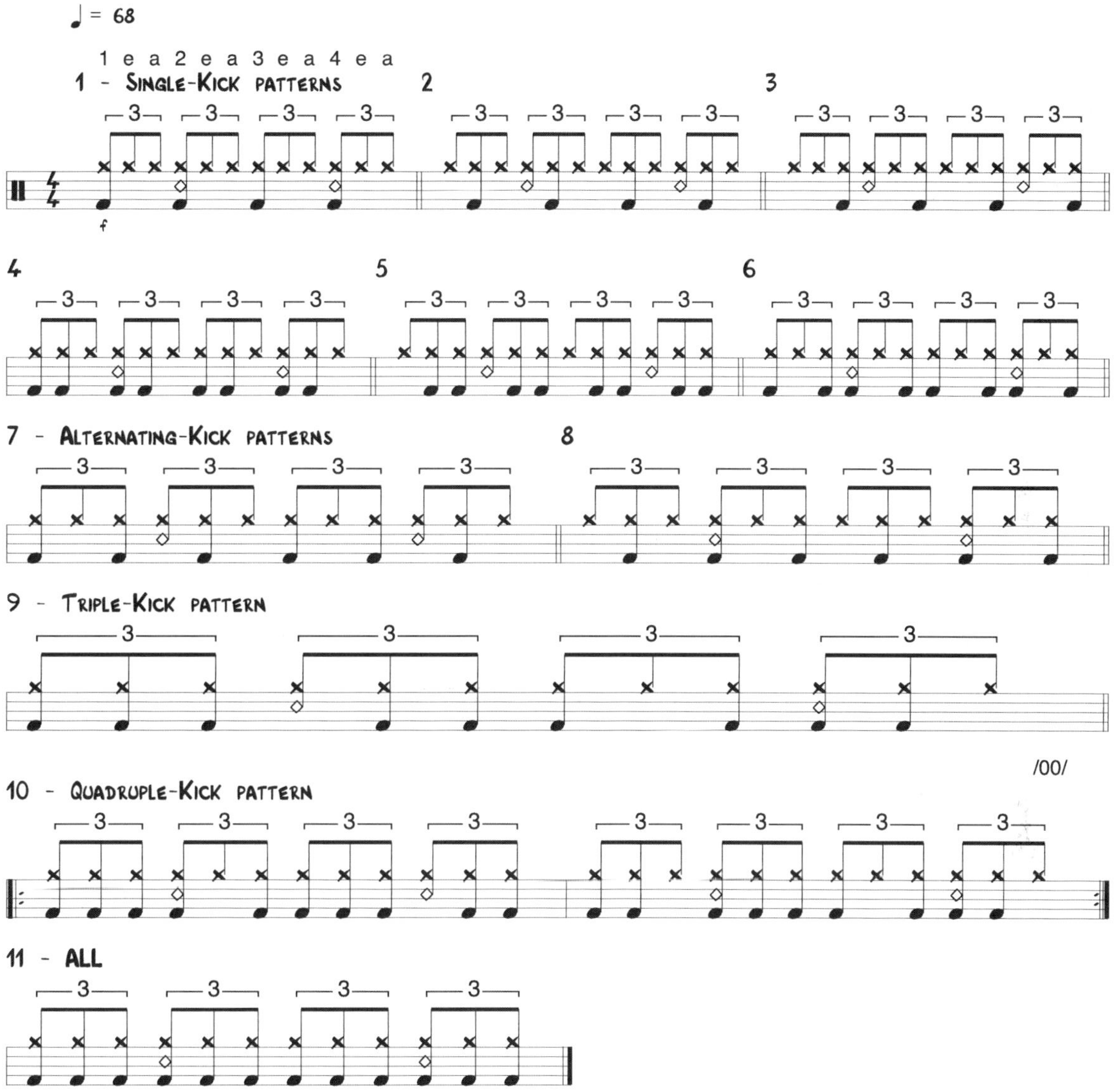

♩ = 68

1 e a 2 e a 3 e a 4 e a

1 - Single-Kick patterns 2 3

4 5 6

7 - Alternating-Kick patterns 8

9 - Triple-Kick pattern

/00/

10 - Quadruple-Kick pattern

11 - ALL

1.4 - All Shuffle Rhythms

Page Instructions

These are based on *1.2 - All 8th Note Triplet Beats*, as was the previous exercise (1.3). It consists of all possible places you could place the kick drum. The purpose is to create a basic coordination that will be carried into the intermediate and advanced stages. It will create a foundation for the student's future drumming.

The tempo is set to 80bpm, which I find to be fairly moderate for any beginner student. If you see this symbol: "**/00/**" above any notes, it means "look" or "watch." It is, laughably, a pair of ascii glasses. For example, the last note of the Quadruple-Kick Pattern is missing a fourth note in the kick drum pattern. This is purposeful; otherwise in order to repeat the pattern, I'd have had to write out a total of five measures (because it is a pattern of 5ths). As a side note, it is important to realize some simple music-math. When the student gets into the intermediate Odd Meter exercises the following will make some more sense. But for now, just know this formula: (4) measures of 5/4 = (5) measures of 4/4. The same goes for 7/4, 9/4 or anything odd-time. It takes five measures of 4/4 to rotate around if you are playing 5/4 over top of it, and vice-versa. Don't worry. It will make sense later on.

All of the shuffle exercises were intended to repeat. If you see a bar repeat sign, it means everything within that section must be repeated. Specifically, the first and sixth measures in this section will be used in the future for songs, so be on the lookout.

Weekly Assignment week #1

- **Exercises**: Lines #1, 2, 3, 4 & 7 – Skip lines 4 & 5 for now. You will need to practice each **measure** for at least **five minutes a day**. Each line contains two or three measures. You should be putting in an hour a day for this exercise. The objective is to be able to perform them without the aid of counting, or without looking at the sheet music (except to know *what* to play). Keep your eyes closed during your practice if you want to really test yourself. And don't worry, these will become natural after awhile.
- **Song**: Begin learning either *Wagon Wheel* (or) *Blue Jeans Blues* or both if you wish. In either song, focus on the X-stick during the verses. Just learn the verses for now, in either case.

Keep a Slow Tempo!

I recommend obtaining a good **slow-down software/app** to assist you in learning new material. You can slow any song down to the speed you need in order to play along. Although *Blue Jeans Blues* is slow, initially keeping the tempo is often difficult for a beginner. You will absolutely require the assistance of your instructor to guide you through the process of learning any song. Learning them by yourself is possible, learning by ear is possible. Getting it right and using it to your advantage requires experience that you simply do not have right now. Please take my advice and **allow an experienced instructor to guide you through all these songs in this curriculum**!

Weekly Assignment week #2

- **Exercises**: Lines 4 & 5. While it is not important to know these blindfolded, it is important to know at least how to play them. You should not expect to get the feel for it just yet. We are just starting. It's okay.
- **Song:** You should be into the chorus sections of each song by now, which include a light snare rimshot (not loud). They are not rock songs. You will **not** need to be able to play every note of these songs, nor learn the entire songs. For now, it's just about skill building.

1.4 - All Possible Shuffle Rhythms

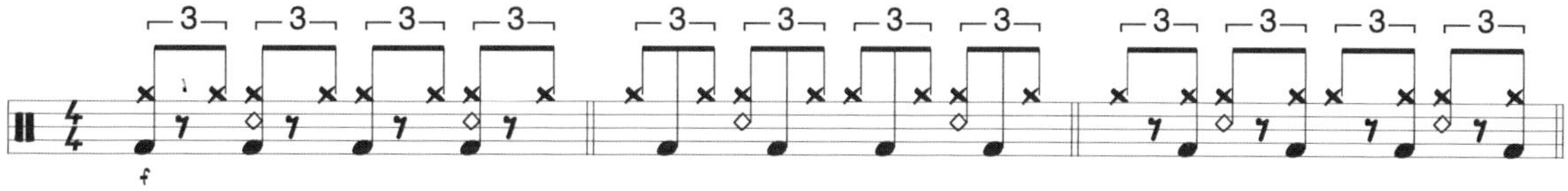

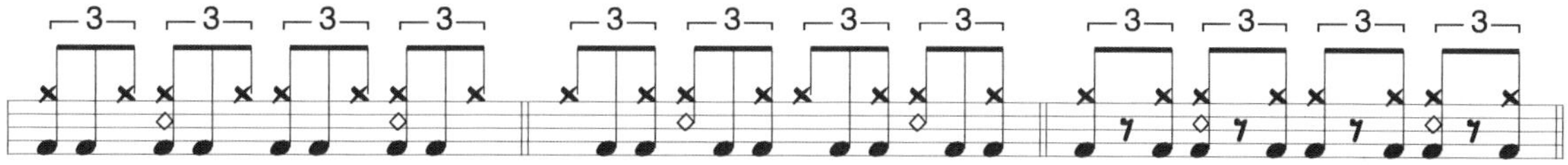

(with all kick triplets)

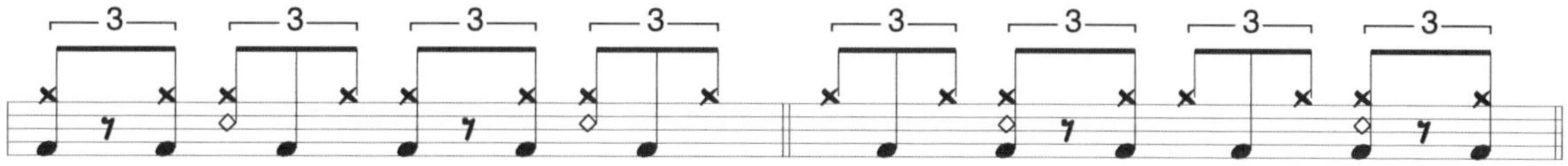

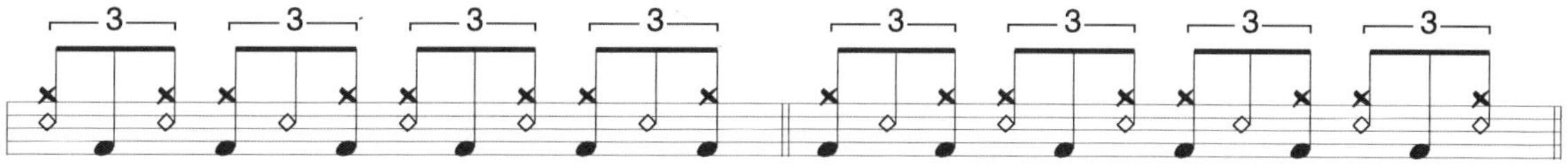

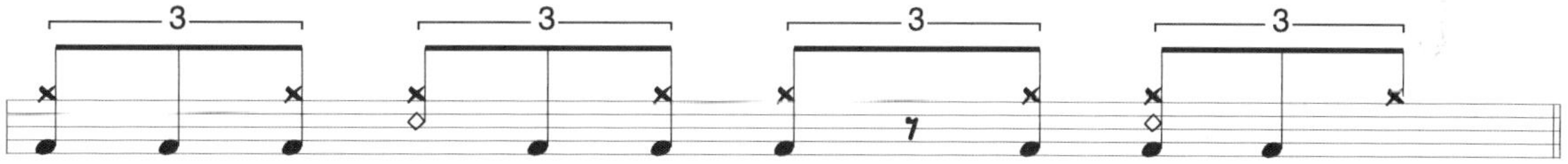

♩ = 80

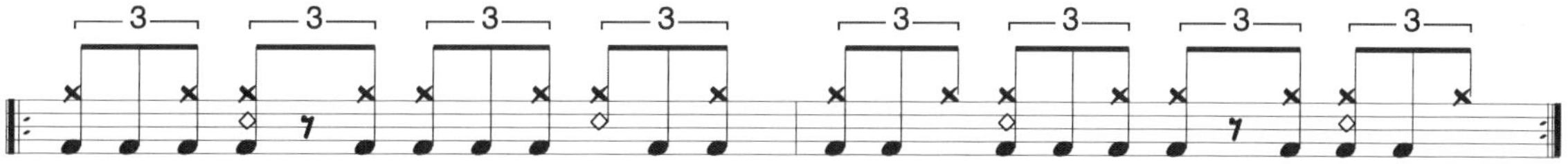

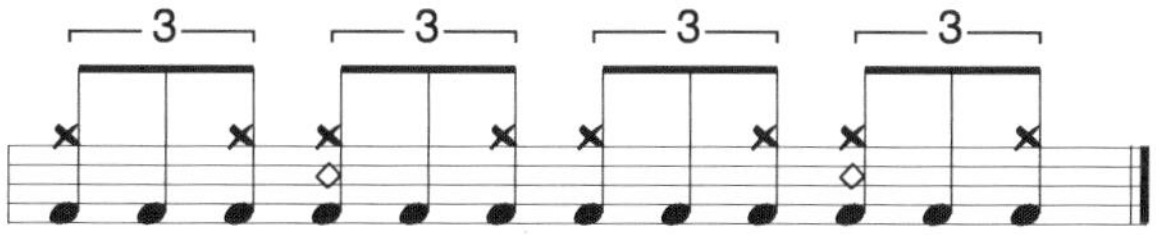

1.5 - All 16th Note Beats

Page Instructions

This page was included in the beginner section although it is used in all stages. **I** still use this page. This is my diligent effort to stress the importance of it, and of the "1.2 - All 8th Note Triplet Beats" page. Please note: **you cannot overuse this page**. You cannot ever learn every possible combination well enough. You cannot find a greater source of constant learning – if you are creative enough with it.

As a Beginner

Learning to recognize each of the patterns, or at least how to count them, is the point. I have never pushed a beginner very far in this section, rather I always return to it at some point. As a beginner student, of course, everyone wants to learn a song. The problem is that the drums are usually the backbone of all songs they want to learn! While in learning piano or any stringed instrument the instructor will almost immediately start in learning songs, (with rare exception) it just cannot be done right away as a beginner drum student. The drumkit is a far more complex instrument that requires all body parts, a basic capacity to count, read music, keep a solid rhythm, focus on technique and timing, and be able to put together some of the prime constructs that create a drum rhythm … all before the first basic song can be played. Still, to play songs is a respectable basic urge. So, no beginner student wants to learn every possible way to play an eight or sixteenth note. Don't bore the student, but don't give into every primal desire to play a tune without first learning the necessary constructs. That's the message.

In this assignment you will find dotted notes and dotted rests. The value of a dotted note is explained in Section 1(i) - *How To Read Dotted Notes.* But a dotted note basically means that the note is worth its value + half its value. Or, differently stated, it is worth (3) of the higher value. So, a dotted eighth note is worth (3) sixteenth notes (e.g., "*1e&*" is the same as a dotted eighth that begins on "1"). Have your instructor assist you if you need help in this area.

As an Intermediate

Begin exploring this page using simple constructs such as playing the hi-hat on quarter beats and reading the exercises as a kick drum like this (figure 25):

Figure 25

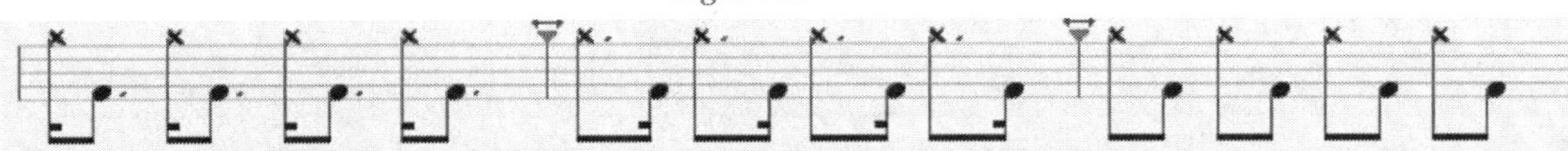

Notice how each of the kick drums are based on the "1.5 - All 16th Note Beats" page. You can change it up by swapping the hi-hat and kick drum like this (figure 26):
Literally, you are limited only by your imagination and determination.

Figure 26

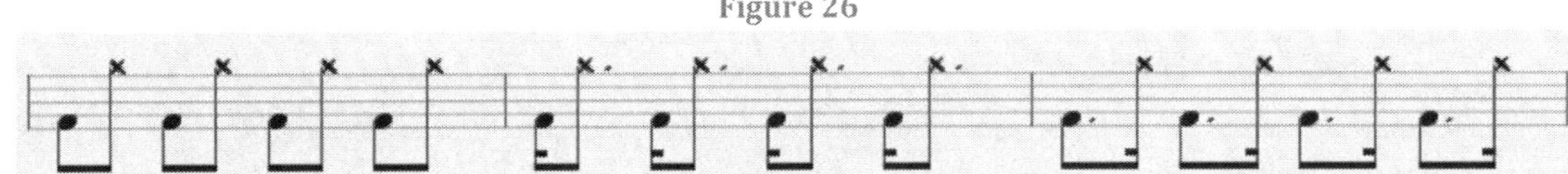

As an advanced student you can begin playing random rhythms with kick and snare, and read this as the hi-hat, or the left hand, or however you want to do it. You are the only one who can set your limitations. This process can easily consume an hour of your time before you realize it. That's good.

Weekly Assignment

- **Learn** to count each of the exercises. Be careful to understand note values and rest values (what they *occupy* in the measure). Next, count while playing the kick drum to these notes.

- Rudiment: The Double-Stroke Roll (figure 27) is another foundational rudiment without which you cannot perform most of the intermediate material. The principles behind it are:
  1) Allow the stick to bounce/rebound – two hits per strike. This will take time to learn properly and requires the aid of your drum instructor;
  2) it should sound smooth – no breaks or "holes" between notes – and should be evenly spaced;
  3) keep the stick between the thumb and the middle finger at slow speeds.

Learn it by practicing this routine over and over:

Figure 27

You should notice is that your wrists and arms move the drum using a consistent pattern of R-L-R-L.

1.5 - All Possible 16th Note Beats

♩ = 80

1 2 3 4 e e e e

SINGLE-NOTE PATTERNS

f

& & & & a a a a

1 e e &

DOUBLE-NOTE PATTERNS

& a 1 a

1 e & e & a

TRIPLE-NOTE PATTERNS

1 & a 1 e a

1 & e a

8TH NOTE AND 16TH NOTE PATTERNS

1 e & a

DOTTED 8TH NOTE PATTERNS

February 22, 2014 – Georgia Red Clay – Rock N Country, Ackworth, GA

LEVEL TWO:
BEGINNER CONCEPTS (WHITE BELT)
GROOVES AND EXERCISES

2.1 - Swing Basics

Page Instructions

Based on the "1.2 - All 8th Note Triplet Beats" page, in these exercises the student will learn the most rudimentary ways to play swing style. A few important items to remember: 1) the kick and snare (in swing) are the melody makers; the ride and hi-hat **foot** together are the rhythm makers. If you can keep the hi-hat foot and ride going (exercise #1), you can keep a swing band going; 2) keep the snare quiet for now (ghost notes) by merely tapping the center of the snare with the stick; 3) play the ride quietly (observe the *mf* at the beginning of the score); 4) play the hi-hat foot hard enough to hear it as well as the ride; 5) play the kick drum using the heel-down (or) toe-only method, which will allow a quiet performance ("feather" the kick drum). That is jazz, for the most part, and learning these dynamics is an essential part of this curriculum!

Counting: "**1 e a 2 e a 3 e a 4 e a**." Notice that the time signature is 4/4 (= 4 quarter notes in each measure). You must count each note and each rest, regardless. Many students forget to count the rest notes and end up playing this as a *straight* 4/4 beat, without the *swing* feel. However, it is a **triplet** beat. By now, you should be familiar with the idea of triplets. We have focused on them for weeks now in order to get you prepared for this part of the curriculum. You are ready. I promise. But in the beginning you must **count, count, count and count.**

The most difficult measures are where the kick is on "e." For some reason, these are very problematic for the brain because playing it there feels disjointed. Just learn them once, build the basic coordination and move on.

Count "1 e a 2 e a 3 e a 4 e a" throughout the entire assignment. Do not stop counting at this stage. You will need the support created by counting to help you develop a certain level of comfort with it. You should spend at least 10 to 15 minutes a day on each measure. Aspire for at least four hours per week in practice. Always. Minimum.

Don't skip this section!!

I cannot stress enough how important this basic lesson is. There are so many aspects to learning swing. If the instructor skips it because he does not think it is important, or that it is not practical, that would be depriving the student of a potentially life-changing exposure to a style. You may find, as I have, that you will be surprised at which students have the propensity to learn which styles. They may take from that influence and become absolutely gifted in that area. Don't deprive yourself, or a student, of that opportunity. If you are the student and you choose to skip this or not place any emphasis on it, you will be greatly short-changing yourself.

Introduction to Ratios

—3— Look closely at each grouping of 16th notes in this exercise. You will find that each 16th note group has a bracket over top of it with a number "3" in it. This is a reference saying, "wherever **two** 16th notes previously were, now **three** will occupy the same amount of space *evenly*." So, the ratio for this is 3:2 – that means for every **two** 16th notes, there are now **three**. The same can be done for the space of 8th notes as well, which you shall experience in upcoming lessons. If it was a 5:2 ratio, you would cram five notes in the same space (evenly) and a quintuplet bracket would be over top with a "5" in it instead of a "3."

If you are a beginner, unless otherwise instructed, please only learn the beginner material. When you finish this curriculum, you will be instructed to return to these pages and review the intermediate material.

Weekly Assignment week #1

- **Exercise**: *Basic Swing Rhythm* (no kick drum) – Ensure you count aloud. This is important. Play the feet first (together) while counting, and then add the ride cymbal. Remember also, heel-down on kick pedal. As you become more comfortable, progressively remove the count (not all at once, just in part).

- **Exercise**: #1 only (*Single-Kick Pattern)* – kick drum on each # and each &. Also learn this pattern using LH (by replacing kick drum with the LH).

- Rudiment: The Flam – (figure 28) The flam is a single strike of the drum with both sticks – what makes it a flam is that while both sticks move downward at once one starts at a lower position and strikes a microsecond sooner. The **left flam** begins with the LH in a higher position; the RH begins near the drumhead. Bring both down at the same time. The lower stick should strike first *and quieter* than the other. The **right flam** is with the RH higher and the LH lower. You must practice the right and left flam throughout the week. Alternate them, L then R.

Figure 28

Weekly Assignment week #2

- **Exercise**: #2 & #3 (*Single-Kick Patterns*) – Always learn these patterns with LH also just like last week!

Weekly Assignment week #3

- **Exercise**: #4 thru #6 (*Double-Kick Patterns);* #7, 8 (*Alternating Kick Patterns)*; #9 + LH

Again, learn these rhythms *one beat at a time.* I could repeat myself numerous times each week, but it will still take some time to understand that when done correctly, **this is a proven method** that will work.

1) Play a single beat (however many notes there are)
2) Play the next beat (even if it is a rest note) and *count it*
3) Continue. If you err, simply *continue*. Do not restart. Train the muscles.
4) Eventually put it into rhythm.
5) Do not play past your fastest tempo, so that you will make zero errors (keep it in the green!).
6) After about half a dozen at a super slow tempo, increase speed.
7) Repeat *at that speed* for another half dozen times.

If you followed this procedure then you should have the coordination built to increase speed now.

2.1 - Swing Basics

♩ = 80

1 e a 2 e a 3 e a 4 e a

BASIC SWING RHYTHM

mf

1 e a 2 e a 3 e a 4 e a 1 e a 2 e a 3 e a 4 e a 1 e a 2 e a 3 e a 4 e a

1 - (BEGINNER) SINGLE PATTERNS 2 3

4 - DOUBLE-PATTERNS 5 6

7 - ALTERNATING PATTERNS 8

9 - ALL

10 - (INTERMEDIATE) DOUBLE-STROKE

11 - DOUBLE-STROKE SNARE/KICK

12 - (ADVANCED) TRIPLE-KICK PATTERN

/00/

13 - QUADRUPLE-KICK PATTERN

2.2 - 6/8 Exercises

Page Instructions

The student is now entering a new phase of counting in three's. In prior assignments the student counted "1ea2ea3ea4ea." Those are counted and written in triplets. Building upon those concepts, the student will now in a count 6/8 time signature. Again, that is (6) 8th notes per measure, and is counted "123456." When 16th notes are added in exercise #2, it is counted with an "&" (and) in between each note: 1&2&3&4&5&6&. These **are not triplets.** There is no triplet bracket above them.

Count aloud. After you build the coordination by playing each measure *one beat at a time* (as discussed in Section 1(e) - *Steps to Learning Any Rhythm*), then learn to keep a steady beat so that each number (123456) is evenly spaced.

IF YOU ARE A BEGINNER, unless otherwise instructed, please only learn the beginner material. When you finish this curriculum, you will be instructed to return to these pages and review the intermediate material.

Weekly Assignment week #1

- **Learn:** lines 1 & 2 using the *one beat at a time* method. Very important! Don't rush this. Count aloud through these exercises, as written above each note. You must be able to perform these without aid of the sheet music by the end of the week.

- Rudiment: The Single-Stroke Triplet – (figure 29) Among the most useful rudiments, the triplet is used in all music styles. As described, it's played "**Right**-Left-Right-**Left**-Right-Left" – as alternating 16th notes – with emphasis on each third note. Watching a triplet as a beginner you may think there are doubled strikes somewhere because of the accents, which alternate. But it really is just RlrLrl. Again, be sure to place accents every third beat: Rlr-Lrl. Also, ensure that you are actually playing *triplets* and not: "Rlr<pause>Lrl<pause>. **There is no pause**; there are no missing notes. It is very common for the beginner student to place a phantom rest note between every three strikes. That would make this simply sixteen notes without the "uh/a," which is incorrect. Play these straight without any rest notes.

Figure 29

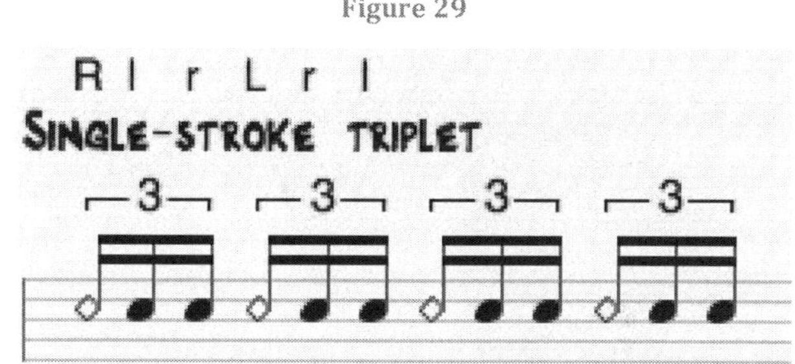

Weekly Assignment week #2

- **Learn:** lines 3 & 4 using the *one beat at a time* method. Remember. RH is ride cymbal in these exercises. Get used to playing the ride gently, which is a skill in and of itself. Count aloud through these exercises, as written above each note. Pay special attention to each 16th note "&" on exercise #4.

- Continue working on Triplets. You should have them to a fairly good tempo by now if you have been working on it steadily for 15 minutes a day.

2.2 - 6/8 Exercises

♩ = 80

1 2 3 4 5 6

1 - Beginner

f

1 2 3 4 5 & 6

2

1 2 & 3 4 5 & 6

3

1 2 & 3 4 5 & 6 & 1 2 & 3 & 4 5 & 6 &

4

5 - Intermediate

6

7

8 - Advanced

9

2.2 - 6/8 Exercises

10

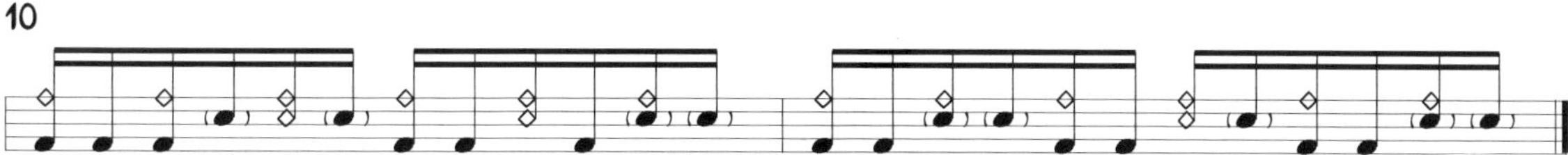

2/2

2.3 - Rock and Funk Beats

Page Instructions

The *Common Rhythms* line, measures #1-4, are basic rhythms used in rock, pop, funk, country, fusion, and just about anything else. They are also the only ones without 16th notes. The idea is to learn some basic rudimentary skills and then build on them, not learn eight thousand different rhythms.

The *16ths Kick* measures cover a number of key concepts such as double (16th note) kick patterns, ghost notes (following and preceding a rimshot), and accented upbeat and downbeat hi-hat patterns (measures 5 & 6). I would recommend combining any two measures for a complete statement, when the student is ready to do so. The third section, *Quarter Note Rock*, requires an open hi-hat.

Remember to play relaxed. Drumming should not be physically painful or even uncomfortable in virtually any way. It should be somewhat aerobic at times, but it never physically strenuous.

Eyes On The Road, Please!

Think of learning music from written material as finding your way to a new location using a GPS. It helps you get there at first. But in order to learn your way there without the GPS, you must begin observing your surroundings ... a tree, a building, a road sign, the way the roads curve ... music is the same way. If we **rely too much upon the written material** we will never *internalize* the feel of the music or the rhythms we are performing. You must spend some time looking at the landscape (eyes off the GPS) by trying to internalize the rhythm you are playing. If you do not do this **then you will never memorize** these ideas and never be able to just play them any time you want. What's the point of that, right?

Weekly Assignment week #1

- **Rhythms:** Begin learning the "Common Rhythms" line (measures #1-4) *with eyes closed.* It is important to learn these rhythms well enough to internalize them – to play them enough that you can call on them at any time, mix them up and make something of your own if you want. But you need to learn them that well. So keep your eyes on the road (off the GPS) after you have understood what to play.

- **Rhythms:** Line 2 (measures #5-7). Pay special attention the accents *on the hi-hat* for measures 5 & 6. Also, the counts are above each measure for any 16th notes. Only count aloud if you need it for learning the material. For this page, constant counting will inhibit you once you have already learned the coordination. No need to memorize these. Exercise #5 would be counted without the hi-hat, in this way: "1--a,2-&-,3---,4---."

- **Song**: The American classic, *Sweet Home Alabama* is ideal for the student to learn at this stage. It consists of everything learned up to this point, plus a few extras. Learn the Intro and Verse only. Try to play it exactly as written.

Weekly Assignment week #2

- **Rhythms:** Continue on to measures #8-16. Again, memorization is **not** necessary. However, if you are progressing quickly it would be good to memorize a few of them. This is where you will begin using *ghost notes* in these rhythms. Please learn to create a big difference between ghost notes and rim shots. Ghost notes are as quiet as you can possibly get them (*ppp to p*). Rimshots are about mid-way loud (*f*) to super loud (*fff*).

- Rudiment: The Drag Triplet – (Figure 30) is a fundamental skill that you will use in upcoming assignments; get familiar with it. The drag triplet is counted "1ea**&**ea-2ea**&**ea" because they are usually played as 16th notes, not 8th notes. The "e,a" counts are with only one hand, and the "#,&" counts are with the other hand: rll (or) lrr. You are going to practice it both ways. Disclaimer: *the name "drag triplet" is not a standardized name, nor is this a standardized rudiment. I insist that it is a rudiment, however, because it is necessary to learn and because no other combination of rudiments will teach it to you.*

You will practice it using the following sticking, and then reverse that sticking when you are ready (figure 30):

Be certain that you are using the "bounce" technique you learned in the double-stroke roll. Let the stick do the work for you. Do not force two strikes with one hand. Doing so will cause you grief at higher speeds.

Figure 30

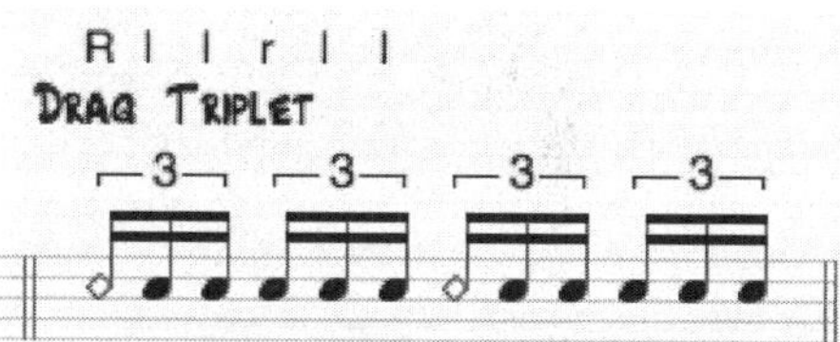

- **Song**: *Sweet Home Alabama* – Chorus. Watch for the "4e" accents after each fourth measure. Go to the second verse. There are some differences. Play them exactly as written.

Weekly Assignment week #3

- **Rhythms:** Continue on to measures #17-23. Remember the hi-hat is played as a rock-style hi-hat. That is, open it up almost all the way. Be sure to tilt your bottom hi-hat cymbal using the knob underneath it on the stand. This will give it the "crash" sound necessary for rock.
    - If you are bold and feel like some "extra credit" try measure #24. The count is above the notes, however there is no way to count in 32nd notes, so watch out!

- **Song**: Continue on the last Chorus and Lead sections of *Sweet Home Alabama*. This is one of the few songs that this curriculum will have you finish all the way through.

Weekly Assignment week #4

- **Rhythms:** Return to the first rhythm. You will need to learn to convert these straight rhythms into a *swing feel*. You are going to return to this idea in section 3.6 *Funk Exercises*. For now, know that the first two are in **eight-note = triplet feel**. The rest of the exercises include some 16th notes. Those sixteenth notes will have a *doubled* swing feel. Please speak to your instructor about how to do this. The videos that accompany this section will demonstrate how they should feel.

2.3 - Rock and Funk

♩ = 110

1 - Common rhythms 2 3 4

1 & a (Look - accents!) 1 e & 2 & a 4 e &
5 - 16ths Kick 6 7

1 & a 1 & a 2 & a 1 e & 2 & a
8 9 10

1 & a 2 & a 1 & 2 e & 3 & a 4 e &
11 12 13

1 & a 2 1 e & 2 e & a 3 & a 4 & 1 & 2 & a 3 e & a 4 & a
14 15 16

17 - Quarter Note Rock 18 19

1 & a 4 e
20 21 22

1 a 2 a 1 a * 2 a
23 24 (32nd notes) extra credit!

2.4 - Alternating 16ths and Alternate Sticking

Page Instructions

Expect to spend two to three weeks on these exercises. It is important to get them up to speed. In the coming months, you will use the skills you'll derive from virtually every one of these measures. Measures 1 & 2 are very common 16th note hi-hat rhythms. The student should aim to bring this up to the speed indicated on the page, which is 110bpm. Proper wrist and finger technique are important. At slow speeds, using just arms or just wrists might work. But once at faster tempos that is no longer viable. Using fingers wherever possible will allow for greater ease, comfort and speed in performance, especially when it comes to 16th note hi-hat rhythms that can get up to 130bpm or faster. Learning to move the left stick *underneath* the right stick from time to time will help also, when moving it from snare to hi-hat.

The intent behind these exercises goes beyond simply learning alternating sticking. The purpose is to teach the beginner the basics of moving around the kit with more ease. For instance, exercise #4 begins with the left stick. Why? Because it ended with two right sticks. Sure, these can be played another way. But the point of the exercise is *economy of motion*. **Wherever the sticking is not written** (such as the first half of measure #5), you will use alternating sticking (rlrlrlrl); wherever it is otherwise listed you will follow it exactly.

Notice that #6 and #7 are essentially the same idea: right hand plays ride and snare in #6; right hand plays hi-hat and snare in #7. What is alike or different between #8 & #9? Look carefully. Sometimes switching a rhythm around will challenge your coordination. And lastly, #10 explores alternate sticking altogether.

Alternate vs. Alternating

Yes, there is a difference between them! Alternating sticking is always rlrlrlrl. We can call this the normal sticking. *Alternate* sticking means using something different than the normal sticking. For instance, in #8 you may naturally want to use the left stick for the snare and play it alternating rlrlrlrl. But the way I've written it will free up your right hand. Playing cross-handed can sometimes restrict your grow and your performance. You will need to learn to play more *economically* in order for your drumming to feel more comfortable.

Switching sticking positions (crossing sticks) during an alternating sticking can be tricky. You will need an instructor to show you the easiest way to do this without causing a collision of your sticks. Try one hand at a time – play only the left-handed part first, then only the right-handed part – and get each one correct and comfortable. This is the way many piano students learn.

If you are left-handed but use a right-handed drumkit, you will need to use *alternate* sticking to perform many songs. These exercises will help you.

Hi Hat Openings

This section is to prepare you for upcoming exercises and songs that you will be learning. It is not essential to learn all of these. For instance, #15 still gives me problems at times, as it is not commonly used. But if you look closely at the lower (foot) hi-hat note you will find these to be especially challenging. But you will need to learn: #11, 12 and #16 for future songs in this curriculum.

Understanding stroke rolls

A "stroke roll" is quantified according to how many "strokes" (hits) the stick makes. A five-stroke roll has five strokes; a seven-stroke has seven. It's really that simple. The last hit is usually going to be a single accent while the others are double-strokes. A simple way to understand how to quickly play any number stroke roll is this: A five-stroke roll has a "double-double-single" that makes five hits. Forget the last hit. Only count the doubles for now (double-double = rr-ll). That is four hits … divided by two movements of the hands/arms is … two. So, the hand/arm motions are: RLR, the last one being an accent, the first two are doubled: RrLlR. A seven-stroke roll is the same: remove the last one and divide as 6/2 = three hits (three double-strokes) and then an accent. 9-stroke roll is: 8/2 = 4 double-strokes + 1 hit RLRL-R. A 21-stroke roll is; 20/2 = 10 double-strokes + 1 hit. After you figure that out, stroke rolls seem a lot less intimidating.

Weekly Assignment week #1

- **Measures:** #1-4 – learn them at least up to 90bpm. Learn these slowly, as always. *Learning perfectly means no mistakes*. However long it takes to stop and get the next note correct, take your time – train your muscles. Muscle memory is key.
    - **On measure #2**, you will need to learn from your instructor how to cross your LH *under* your RH to create a smooth transition on the "uh/a" beat of "3." Learn to sweep the left hand from snare to hi-hat without any arm motion first. Just tap the hi-hat, then the snare, repeat. There is no arm motion. When you add RH back into the rhythm you will find where the LH crosses under the RH when playing the hi-hat.

- **Song**: *Wonderful Tonight* – begin learning this classic Eric Clapton song that uses alternating 16th note hi-hat. Learn only the Intro section and the verse. There is special emphasis in the hi-hat part, emphasizing the "-&a#" feel. The "e" is there, but played quietly, as a ghost note. There is an accent on each "#" of the count.

- Rudiment: Five-stroke roll – (figure 31) practice this all week, preferably on a practice pad, for about 15 minutes at a time. USE THE BOUNCE technique or this will be troublesome. It should feel physically easy to do.

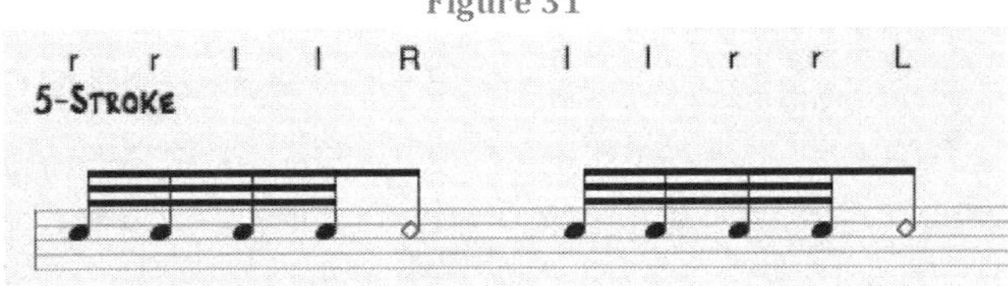

Figure 31

Weekly Assignment week #2

- **Measures:** #5-10. Remember, anything that does not have the sticking above it is *alternating* rlrlrlrl.

- **Song**: *Wonderful Tonight* – Have you noticed the *double measure* repeats as well as the bar repeats? These are certainly important to pay attention to in transcriptions.

  One means "repeat the last two measures as they were played" (double measure repeat) and the other means "repeat these measures from the beginning" (bar repeat).

- Rudiment: Seven-stroke roll – (figure 32) Practice this rudiment all week. Again, it should feel comfortable, not strained. Practice one side, then the other (not all at once as written). Practice first rrllrrL and then llrrllR separately.

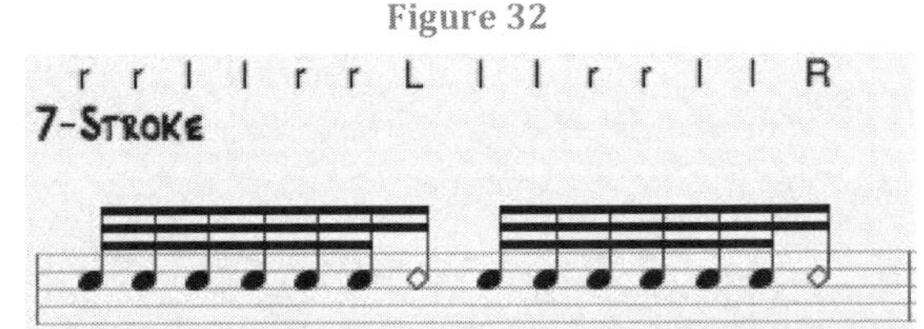

Figure 32

Weekly Assignment week #3

- **Measures:** Hi-hat openings – all of them. Focus on Measures #11 & 12. You will be using these in the coming songs.

- **Song**: *Wonderful Tonight* – finish the entire song. Be able to play this song without aid of sheet music, up to the speed that is listed on the transcription.

- Rudiment: Nine-Stroke Roll – (figures 33 & 34) Practice this rudiment all week. By now, you should know how to subdivide (9 strokes divided by 2 hand/arm strokes equals 4 double-strokes).

  Figure 33

  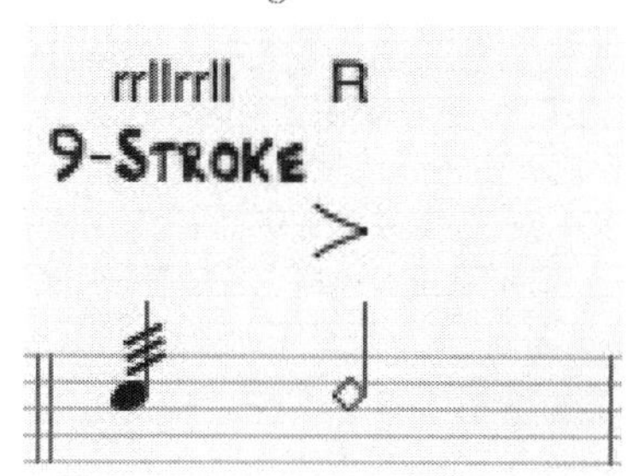

  Notice that it is written differently. This is how stroke rolls are written in snare solo music. You are going to see this again so let me explain. The hash marks on the snare note mean to interpret this as a 32nd note because there are three of them. See the seven-stroke roll in last weeks lesson? See it has three bar lines? That means 32nd note also. The sticking is written over top of the hashed note in this rudiment (rrllrrll) so you would recognize how to play it. If you were to *remove the hash mark*, then it would be played as "1 (&) 2" where you hit only on "1" and on "2."

It could also be written this way and it would mean the same thing:

Figure 34

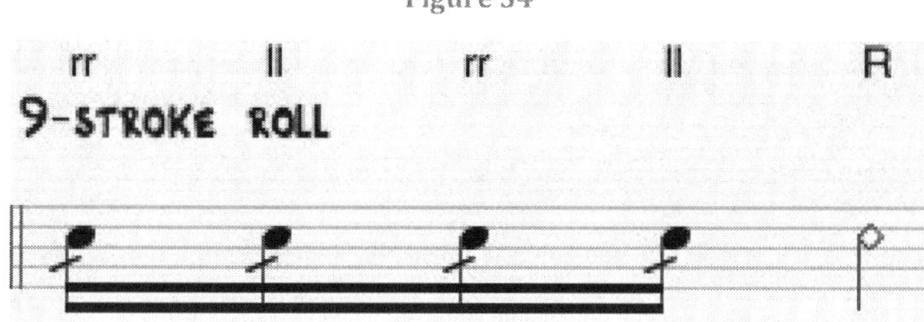

That is because there are still three bars on each note. The 16th note bars, plus one hash = three bars = 32nd notes.

2.4 - Alternating 16ths & Alternate sticking

Beginner

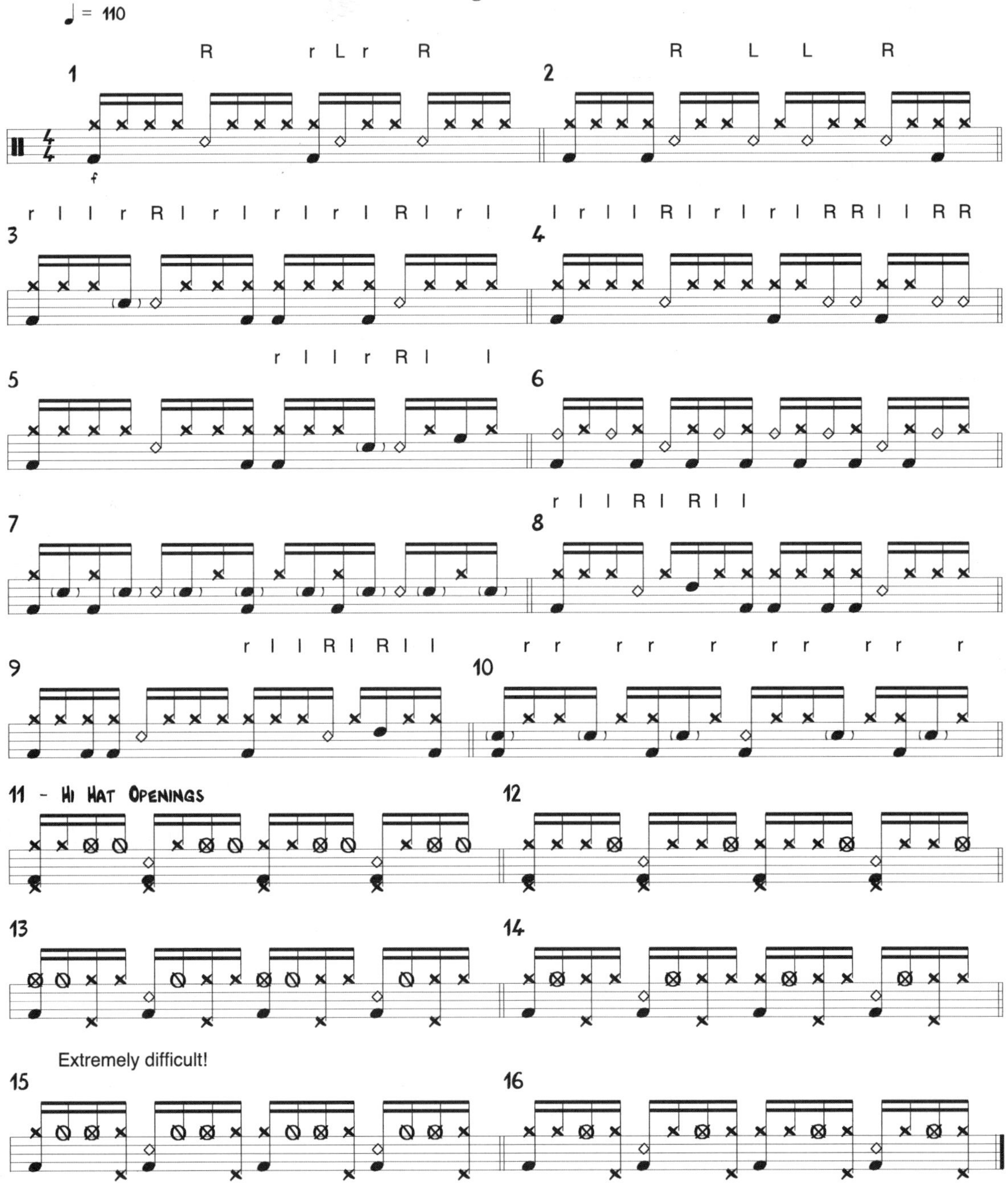

♩ = 110

R r L r R
1

R L L R
2

r l l r R l r l r l r l R l r l
3

l r l l R l r l r l R R l l R R
4

r l l r R l l
5

6

7

r l l R l R l l
8

r l l R l R l l
9

r r r r r r r r r r
10

11 - Hi Hat Openings

12

13

14

Extremely difficult!
15

16

2.5 - *Open Hi Hat Reading Exercises*

Page Instructions

The foot exercises at the top of the assignment will help at first – knowing "both, left, right" is the quickest way to learn the proper coordination for these measures: 1) count each measure, of course.; 2) think of them as "both" or "left" or "right," as written; 3) add the hi-hat and then the snare. The first line is intended to create the initial coordination to learn the rest of the page. Ensure you have learned that very well before proceeding.

Play each section straight through, measure after measure, to the end. Line three is especially difficult. The student should not expect to learn the entire thing first time around. S/he should spend two, maybe three weeks on it and move on. Pick up where you left off sometime in the later intermediate stage, after completion of this entire curriculum.

<u>If you are a beginner</u>, unless otherwise instructed, please only learn the beginner material. When you finish this curriculum, you will be instructed to return to these pages and review the intermediate material.

Weekly Assignment week #1

- **Learn:** Line #1 (foot exercises) – Simply learn to negotiate how the left foot works with the right foot.
- **Song**: *Smoke On Water* – Begin with line #2 of the Intro section where the Hi-Hat enters. Focus on the accents on each quarter note. The Hi-hat should be slightly loose, not too tight.
- <u>Rudiment</u>: Six-Stroke Roll – (figure 35) This rudiment is different than the other stroke-roll rudiments in that the standard six-stroke is played with the doubles *inside* of the single strikes. Of course, any arrangement of six strokes is a six-stroke roll, technically. But this is the standard. Both ways of writing this rudiment are provided for you in figure 35. The second one without the hash marks would be played as: 1e-a 2e-a. The accents tell you to put emphasis on *only* those notes. Learn it the first direction, R llrr L and then the other direction, L rrll R. The last note and the first note should sound like they are together.

Figure 35

Weekly Assignment week #2

- **Learn:** Line #2 – work slowly through the measures, *one beat at a time*. Remember: perfect practice means **stop, see, study, strike**. Don't assume how to play what comes next any more than you would assume what is on the next page of a book. Create muscle memory.
- <u>Rudiment</u>: Swiss-six roll – (figure 36) is a basic rudiment similar to the *six-stroke roll*, which you just studied. They are very similar. One is a triplet feel, the other is not, but they are the same sticking. **Be sure to play it in *triplet feel***! The biggest mistake new students make is to

Figure 36

play this as a straight feel! The second is to forget to connect the last note and the first one!

- **Song**: *Smoke On Water* – Complete the Intro and Bass Guitar sections before the end of the week, including the 6-stroke roll fill.

Weekly Assignment week #3

- **Learn:** Line #3 – This line is tricky. You may stop after this line, or if you are finding it easy, then continue on, noticing the repeat bars.

- **Song**: *Smoke On Water* – Study the Verse section. You should be able to play the two fills at the end of the 2nd and 4th pass *very slowly.* No one expects it to be up to speed. Keep working on it.

2.5 - Open Hi Hat Reading Exercises

Play straight through

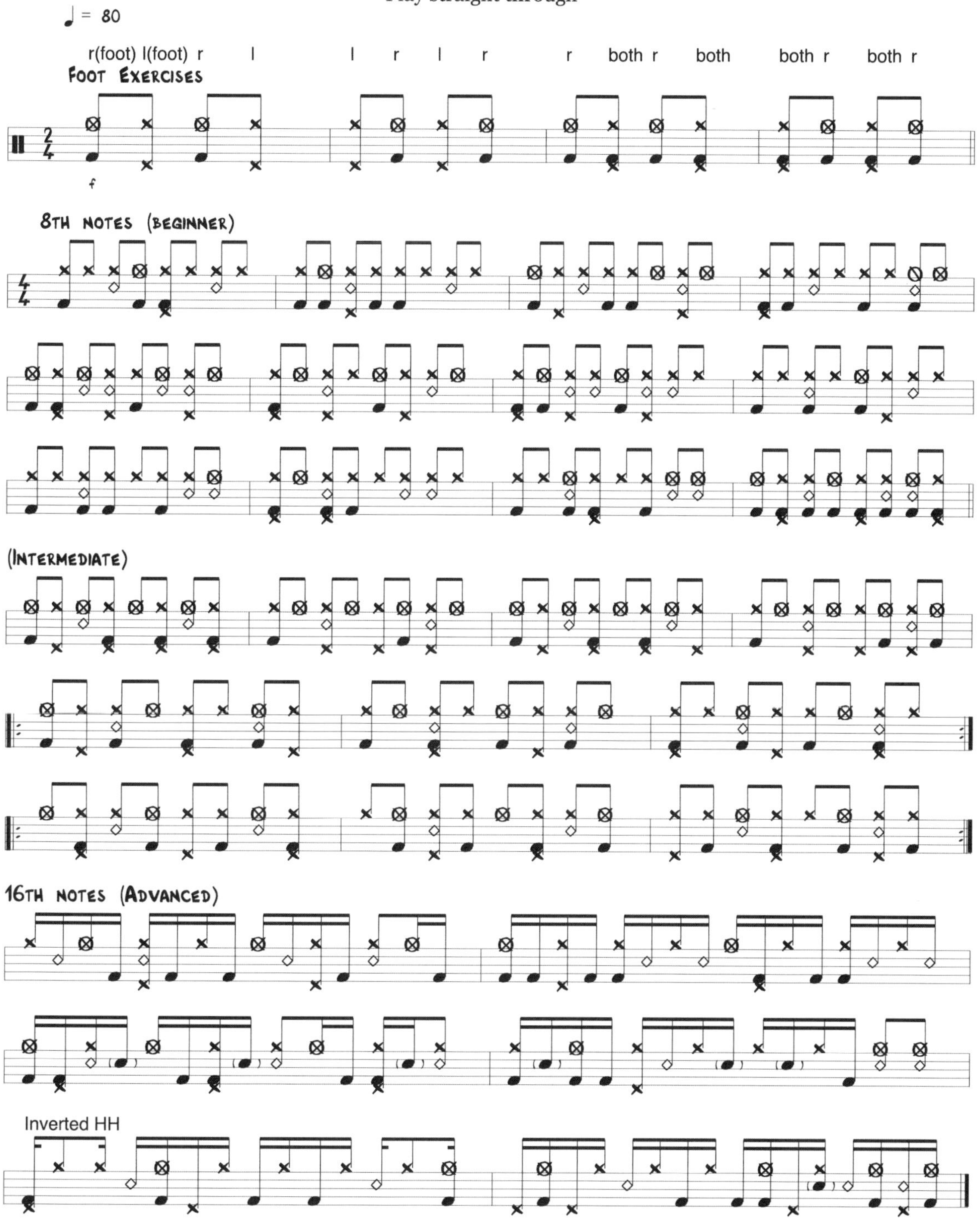

♩ = 80

r(foot) l(foot) r l l r l r r both r both both r both r

FOOT EXERCISES

8TH NOTES (BEGINNER)

(INTERMEDIATE)

16TH NOTES (ADVANCED)

Inverted HH

2.6 - Triplet rhythm Reading Exercise

Page Instructions

After assignment 2.5, this should be simple to play. The point is not to develop technique or to develop coordination. The point is to be able read all the way through without stopping. All you need to know is that the kick drum note shifts every eleventh eighth note. Just be able to read it all without stopping.

Weekly Assignment

- **Learn:** You should be able to play the entire thing without issue by the end of the week. Just read from beginning to end.

- **Song**: *The Sky is Crying* – Just learn the Chorus (line one) for now. The ride cymbal should be played on the center of the cymbal, not on the bell. This is a 12-bar blues ballad. It has a swing (tripletized) feel. There is one section labeled "no swing" – you will hear it. The very end is called a "fermata."

2.6 - Triplet Rhythm Reading Exercise

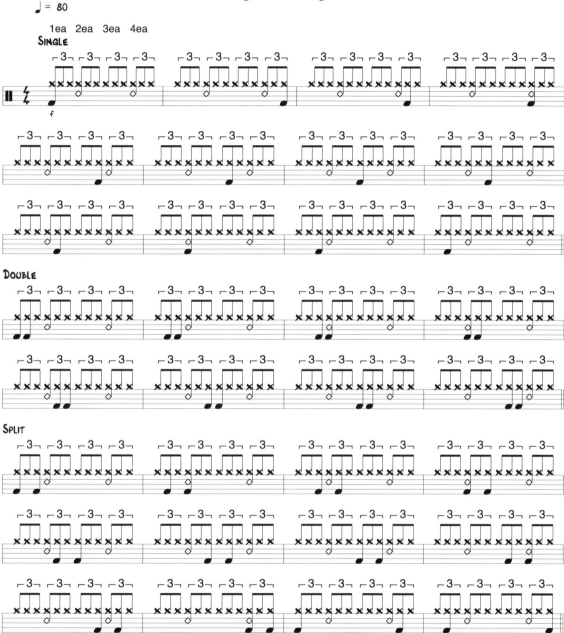

Beginner Reading

♩ = 80

1ea 2ea 3ea 4ea

Single

f

Double

Split

2.6 - Triplet Rhythm Reading Exercise

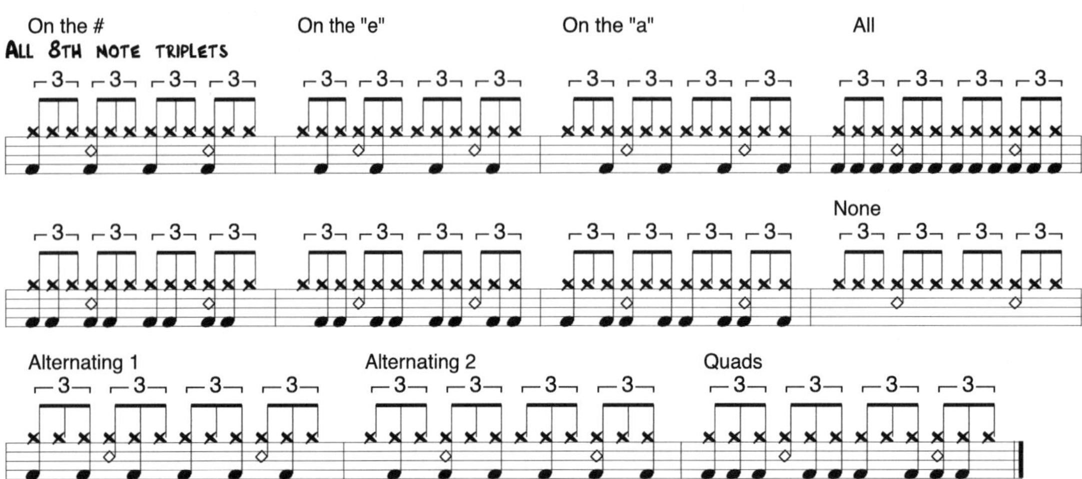

2/2

2.7 - Kick Drum Reading Exercise #1 (8th notes)

Page Instructions

Pick one of the rhythms at the bottom of the page that does **not** have a kick drum pattern. Apply that rhythm to this page starting at line #1. It will be played as an *ostinato* (a repeating rhythm) over top of the rest of the page. This is more than a reading exercise. It is intended to teach the student to automate an ostinato without reading that ostinato, and to establish some essential coordination.

Remember to use this formula:

1) Kick drum only
2) RH + RF
3) LH + RF
4) LF + RF
5) RH + LH
6) RH + LF
7) LH + LF
8) ALL together

Weekly Assignment week #1

- **Learn:** only the first line of this page. Remember to recognize "both, left, right" regarding foot patterns. Start with just the feet: Both, right, left … whatever the pattern is.

- **Song**: *The Sky is Crying* – Learn the Verse section – all twelve measures – including the fills. They are written exactly as they are played on the original. The "<" symbol over the build on the last measure of this line is a *crescendo*, which indicates increasing in volume.

Weekly Assignment week #2

- **Learn:** lines 2 & 3. Your instructor will need to explain to you what the following mean: Da Capo, Da Coda, Segno (the symbol), D.S. al Coda and Coda (the symbol).

- **Song**: *The Sky is Crying* – Learn the remainder of the song. Apply your ear training to learning the other fills in the song.

Weekly Assignment week #3

- **Learn:** the remainder of the assignment. If you have already done so, then simply use an alternate pattern from the bottom of the page.

- **Song:** *Pour Some Sugar On Me* – Learn the first section, the Intro, including the stop at the end of that section. If you find that easy, move on to the Verse section. The online transcription purposefully does not contain the exact fills done by Rick Allen on this song. It is up to you to use your ear training and figure them out.

2.7 - Kick Drum Reading Exercise #1

8th notes
(Play straight through)

♩ = 75

B B L R B L R L B L 1 & 2 3 4 & 1 2 3 4

f

Da Capo

Da Coda

D.S. al Coda

#1 #2 #3

RHYTHMS (SNARE, RIDE, HH)

#4 #5 add splash #6

2.8 - Beginner Snare Solos

Page Instructions

Warning: This is **the painful page**. I'm just going to say that upfront. But it is necessary all the same. Written in the tradition of the great book by Charley Wilcoxon, *The All American Drummer - 150 Rudimental Solos*, these **three simple solos** are designed to utilize most basic rudiments of double-strokes, single and double paradiddles, flams, Swiss-six and various stroke-rolls. Boring however it may be, it is essential in learning basic rudimentary skills, especially for members of middle school or high school band. Sticking matters (R or L)! Look at the sticking atop each beat!

Weekly Assignment week #1

- **Learn:** Solo #1 (easy) – just learn the first line.
- **Song**: Pour Some Sugar On Me – Chorus section

Weekly Assignment week #2

- **Learn:** line 2 of Solo #1
- **Song**: *Pour Some Sugar On Me* – Drums Interlude section

Weekly Assignment week #3

- **Learn:** lines 3 & 4 of Solo #1
- **Song:** *Pour Some Sugar On Me* – Complete the entire song, pay attention to the ending.

2.8 - Beginner Snare Solos

2.8 - Beginner Snare Solos

2/2

Level Three:
Higher Beginner (yellow belt)
Fills, Swing and Funk

3.1 & 3.2 - Paradiddle Drumkit Exercises (Beginner & Advanced)

Page Instructions

As on the rudiments page (adopted from 1985 Percussive Arts Society), there are only four possible **single-paradiddles**, and six double-stroke paradiddles. And since to my knowledge no one has standardized names for all of them, these are the names I have given them: *standard, inverted, reversed, inverted doubles*. For the **double-paradiddles**, there are also: *upbeat standard* and *inverted #2*. The names will make more sense to you after you have learned them. *You need to learn the paradiddles as a rudiment also* in addition to learning them on the drumkit.

I have also segregated the paradiddles into two main categories, whether single- or double-paradiddle: *Linear Hands* and *Linear Hand-Foot*. Both drumset skills are absolutely necessary for this curriculum, and for real-life drumming. Additionally, I have added another page: "3.2 - Paradiddle Fills – Advanced," which is a series of ultimate challenges for you to return to at a later date of your choosing.

The purpose of teaching paradiddles on the drumkit is the aspect of separating the hands – one on the hi-hat and one on the snare, depending upon whether you play "right over left" or "open-handed." Be certain to be obedient to the rimshots and ghost notes in this lesson. At higher speeds it will serve you well. And as always, *learn these slowly*. As a beginner it is not necessary to master any one of these concepts.

Weekly Assignment week #1

- Rudiment: Single Paradiddles – Grab a practice pad because here's where you begin learning one of the most useful rudiments in drumming. It is the most versatile. You will focus more on the *standard* and *inverted* paradiddles because they are the most used, but the others are important as well and will build coordination and give you a greater drumming vocabulary. Focus on the right hand and the rhythm it creates by itself when playing the *standard* paradiddle: 1-&a (2)e. Look at the rudiments page for the sticking of each one.

- **Exercises: Single-paradiddles** – Linear Hands: all – (**lines** 1&2) Notice in the "reversed" measure, you will need to perform a rimshot followed by a ghost note using the same hand. This is an important part of what you will be learning from me in the future.

- **Song**: *Nothing Else Matters* – This is the first song assigned to you in this section, and the first song assigned to you that is a serious drum part. It has a "deep pocket." That means try to hold back playing the snare until the last possible microsecond. Everything on the original is on this chart, note for note. The parts are not hard, and you can memorize them quickly, but it is a reading challenge. For this week, learn the first verse. There is a repeat bar and three alternate endings. An *alternate ending* is how each pass between repeat signs is played differently at the end of each pass. Lars Ulrich wrote hard-hitting and solid drum parts that are not overly complex to learn. Have fun and don't be intimidated. You are ready for this!

Weekly Assignment week #2

- Rudiment: Double-Paradiddles – Again, *standard* and *inverted* are the focus, but learn all six of these at least a little. Become familiar with four of them; know the other two really well. The sticking is important but *remember to use your technique for double-stroke* (bouncing) otherwise you'll languish when speed increases. You won't get passed a certain speed if you use the wrong technique.

- **Exercises: Single-paradiddles** – Linear Hand-Foot: all – (**lines** 3&4) All of these will prepare you for the upcoming assignments in funk, which is rather extensive. You will need to focus on the dynamics of the ghost notes and rimshots. *Be certain with your instructor that you are using the proper techniques* for these exercises. I cannot stress enough that if you are learning them without the "bounce" of the stick instead of driving it into the snare twice, that you will have problems learning other assignments in this curriculum.

- **Song**: *Nothing Else Matters* – Chorus 1 thru Bridge. Watch for the 32nd notes on the sixth measure of the bridge.

Weekly Assignment week #3

- **Exercises: Double-paradiddles** – Linear Hands: standard & inverted **and** Linear Hand-Foot: standard & inverted. The secret to learning these rhythms is to focus on the kick drum pattern.

- **Song**: *Nothing Else Matters* – Verse 3 to end.

3.1 - Paradiddle Drumkit Exercises

Basic

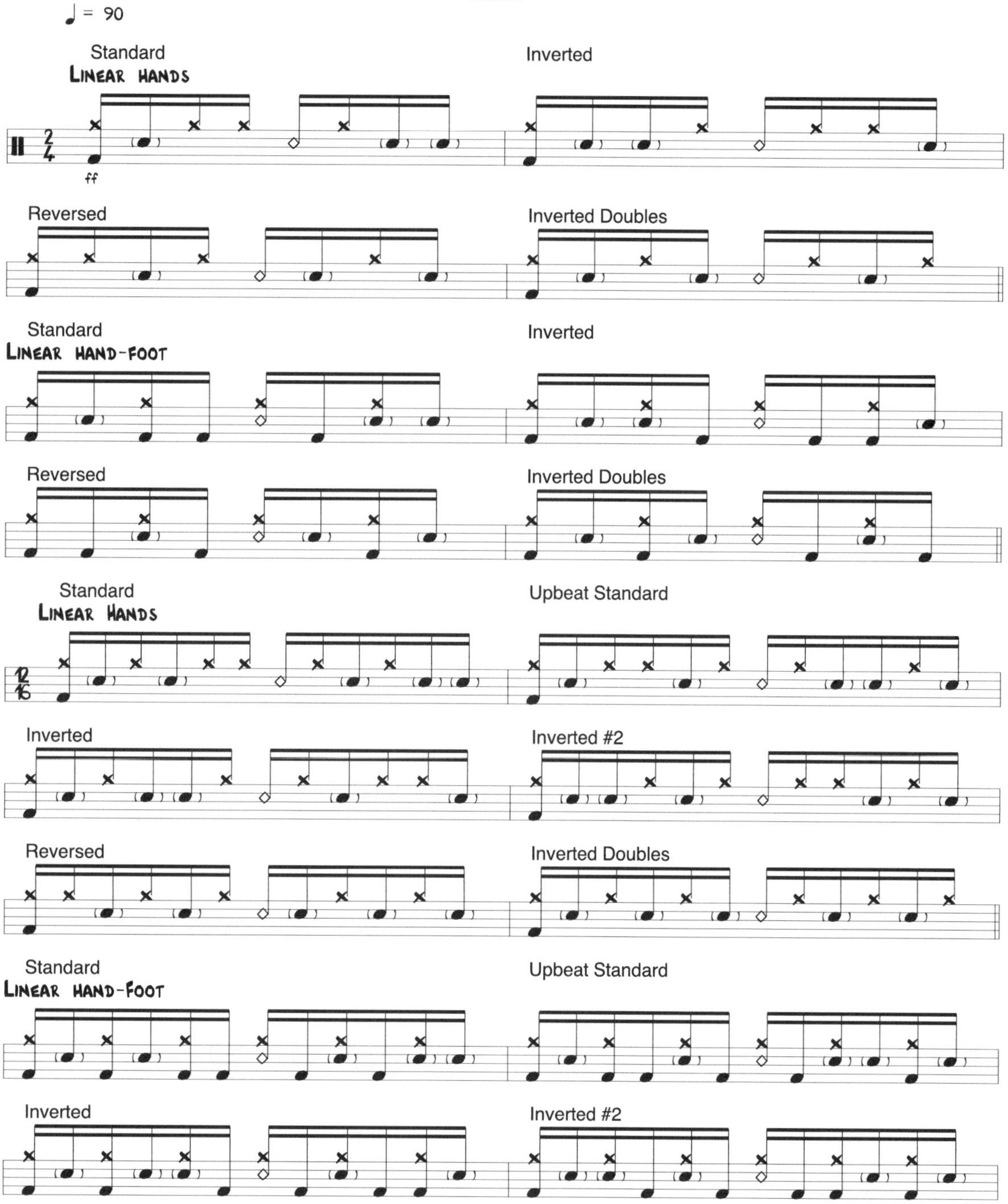

♩ = 90

3.1 - Paradiddle Drumkit Exercises

2/2

3.2 - Paradiddle Drumkit Exercises

Advanced

3.2 - Paradiddle Drumkit Exercises

2/2

3.3 - Inverted Paradiddle Grooves

Page Instructions

The first question I'm sure you have is, "How is this page (grooves) different than the last assignment (exercises)?" Firstly, it's *shorter!* More importantly, I created these rhythms for the intent of exercising your coordination. Additionally … these are based *only* on the inverted paradiddle. It's just a little exercise to exploit some your new paradiddle skills.

Weekly Assignment week #1 (Beginner)

- **Grooves:** #1 & #2 – watch out for the right-handed accent on #2

- **Song**: *Fire* – Learn this exactly as performed by Mitch Mitchell – learn just the Intro and Instrumental sections

Weekly Assignment week #2 (Intermediate)

- **Grooves:** #3 & #4 – watch for the hi-toms in this one. Be sure to maintain the correct sticking throughout: rllr-lrrl

- **Song**: *Fire* – Learn the Verse and Chorus sections. The rest is up to you. Use your ear on the remainder of the song. Listen for fills and rhythm changes.

3.3 - Inverted Paradiddle Grooves

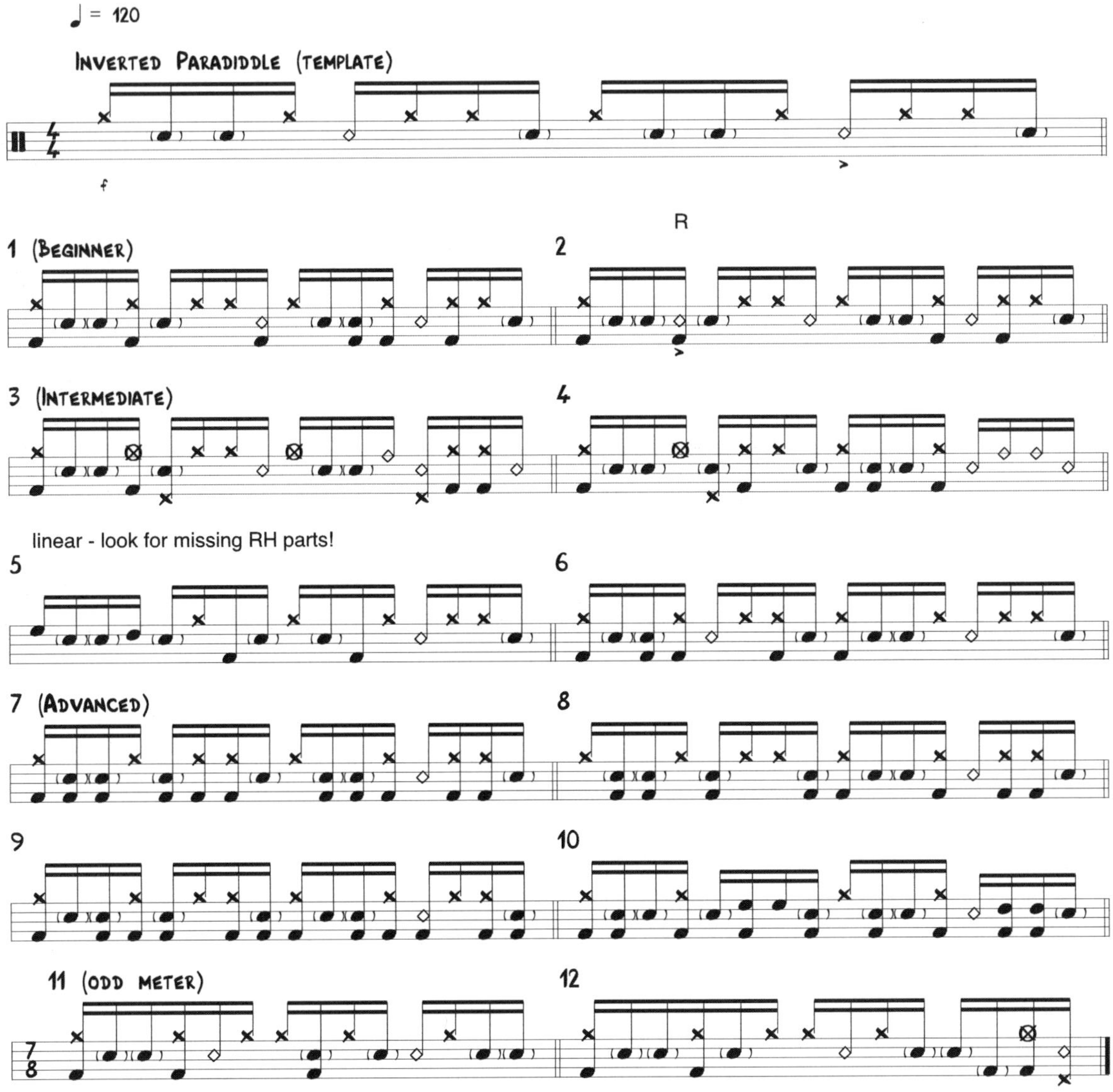

♩ = 120

Inverted Paradiddle (template)

f

R

1 (Beginner)

2

3 (Intermediate)

4

linear - look for missing RH parts!

5

6

7 (Advanced)

8

9

10

11 (odd meter)

12

3.4 - Swing Exercises

Page Instructions

In keeping with the tradition of the great Jim Chapin in the *Advanced Techniques For the Modern Drummer* (which I highly advise every serious drum student to get right away and begin studying), these exercises are fundamental in developing jazz and swing skillsets.

But First, Some History

"Swing", as most rhythms, is a type of dance and comes from the great jazz scene from the late 1920's and 1930's during the Calvin Coolage era of American prosperity. Jazz was powerful, energetic and had a bad social stigma for a long while. But the greatest musicianship of this nation was born from that era, and from this style of music. Jazz began in the late 19th century from what is called "ragtime" music. Lincoln Park was opened in 1902 in New Orleans as a center for ragtime and early jazz performance. In 1917, the Dixieland Jass Band recorded *Livery Stable Blues* and appeared in the movie, "*The Good for Nothing*."

The beginner student should not expect to learn all these rhythms, nor should s/he expect to learn them at any playable speed in a live jazz band. Just use them to build the initial basic skills. Later, you should return to this material to better digest it. I've included a "bonus" at the end that I created while experimenting with fifths within triplets. If you can play it, feel free contact me with a video. I'd love to see how others have applied the idea.

If you are a beginner, unless otherwise instructed, please only learn the beginner material. When you finish this curriculum, you will be instructed to return to these pages and review the intermediate material.

Weekly Assignment week #1 (Beginner)

- **Exercises:** #1 thru #4 – Please notice that the ride cymbal is played throughout these exercises (using the soft part, not the bell), and the hi-hat foot is played on all the "&" notes. They are played softly, even the rimshots.
- **Song**: Continue working on *any* past material.

Weekly Assignment week #2 (Beginner)

- **Exercises:** #5 thru #9
- **Song**: Continue working on *any* past material.

Weekly Assignment week #3 (Intermediate)

- **Exercises:** #10 thru #14 – Watch for accents on the kick drum beginning in #10. The accents are important to learn so that the full melody of these exercises is understood.
- **Song**: Continue working on *any* past material.

Weekly Assignment week #4 (Intermediate)

- **Exercises** #15 thru #18
- **Song**: Continue working on *any* past material.

3.4 - Swing Exercises

Beginner thru Advanced
(Combine random measures)

♩ = 120

1 a 2 a 3 4 a

1 - Beginner

2

mf

3

4

1 a & e a 2 e a & a

5

6

7

8

Note: accented kick drum begins here

9

10 - Intermediate

11

12

13

14

3.4 - Swing Exercises

2/3

3.4 - Swing Exercises

5's in swing
31 - Bonus

3/3

3.5 - Hi Hat Up-beat Exercises

Page Instructions

This begins your experience in hi-hat foot interdependence. You must count (#,e,&,a); you must complete everything on this page. However, you should not expect to master anything, especially the intermediate measures. This page will help strengthen your coordination, but it is not designed for you to memorize. Still, you must be able to play these *without looking* before we can move on. That is the one requirement. Again, do not rely upon the written material. Look, learn and let go. Trust yourself. You must internalize things that you learn. **Stop, see, study, strike.**

There are three sections to this page: 1) hi-hat on "&;" 2) hi-hat on "&-a;" 3) hi-hat on "e-&." It gets more difficult as it progresses.

IF YOU ARE A BEGINNER, unless otherwise instructed, please only learn the beginner material. When you finish this curriculum, you will be instructed to return to these pages and review the intermediate material.

Weekly Assignment week #1 (Beginner)

- **Exercises:** Complete measures #1 thru #8.
- **Song**: *American Idiot* – You are ready for this song! Don't look so intimidated! Take it slow and learn it at half speed, only up through the first verse. Pay attention to the "road signs" like bar and measure repeats and alternate endings. An easy way to determine if you've completed a measure (because this song is so fast) is to count how many "backbeats" (2 & 4) you have hit. **Each measure gets two backbeats**, so that makes it easy to learn where you are. *I advise you* to ask your instructor how to properly read some of this transcript.

Weekly Assignment week #2 (Beginner)

- **Exercises:** Complete measures #9 thru #16.
- **Song**: *American Idiot* – Chorus 1 and Instrumental

Weekly Assignment week #3 (Intermediate)

- **Exercises:** Complete measures #17 thru #24.
- **Song**: *American Idiot* – Verse 2 (notice that the last eight measures are different from the first eight measures!); and Chorus 2.

Weekly Assignment week #4 (Intermediate)

- **Exercises:** Complete measures #25 thru #36.
- **Song**: *American Idiot* – By now you can play the chorus without problem. Finish the rest of the song.

3.5 - Hi Hat Up-beat Exercises

♩ = 80

Single HH (played on "&")

1 - Beginner 2 3 4

5 6 7 8

9 10 11 12

13 14 15 16

Double HH (& a)

17 18 19 20

21 - Intermediate 22 23 24

25 26 27 28

Double HH (e &)

29 30 31 32

33 34 35 36

3.6 - Funk Exercises

Page Instructions

By now you'll begin to notice a pattern in your assignments: **exercises, grooves, song**. The more repetitions you do, the better you will learn and remember these. I have a general rule of 500 repetitions just to get it into muscle memory for a live performance. Sometimes, that's not enough depending upon the complexity of what I'm learning. Also by now, you should begin trying to commit everything you read to memory. You don't want to get stuck relying upon the written material. You need to know how to memorize a rhythm and come back and just know it. It's okay to glance once in awhile at the material to remind you what to play. But after you know what to play, just close your eyes and play it.

From Swing to Straight Feel

This is also where you are going to learn how to change a straight rhythm into a swing/shuffle feel. First, you're going to learn how to change a simple 8th note hi-hat RH pattern into a shuffle. Begin by playing 8th notes on the hi-hat. Count 1&2&3&4&. Now play a shuffle pattern on the hi-hat at the exact same tempo (use a metronome); count 1-a2-a3-a4-a. Now switch back and forth between them. Next, add the snare to the rhythm, on counts 2&4. Then add kick on counts 1&3. Continue this exercise until it is comfortable.

The big step is doubling the swing/shuffle pattern speed. Here's how you do it: 1) play the same shuffle pattern you did, only play the kick only on "1" and the snare only on "3." When you are comfortable with this, 2) straighten it out to a non-swing feel, then return to swing; 3) say aloud "1-a&-a2-a-&" counting all four quarter notes; 4) now double the metronome tempo.

IF YOU ARE A BEGINNER, unless otherwise instructed, please only learn the beginner material. When you finish this curriculum, you will be instructed to return to these pages and review the intermediate material.

Weekly Assignment week #1 (Beginner)

- **Exercises:** #1 thru #4 – pay attention to the ghost notes and rimshots. Ensure your instructor has shown you the best way to perform the doubles on the snare.

Weekly Assignment week #2 (Beginner)

- **Exercises:** #5 thru #7 – #5 has doubles on the snare using both "e&" as well as "&a." Pay attention to where the hi-hat foot is placed in #7.
    - Here's where it gets interesting. I want you to go back to #1 thru #4 and **play them in a swing feel**. When you can do that, do the same to #5 thru #7. The accompanying video to this section will demonstrate how these should feel.

Weekly Assignment week #3 (Intermediate)

- Exercises: #8 thru #12 – Pay attention to the hi-hat foot. #10 is tricky if you are not using the proper technique to allow the stick to bounce.

3.6 - Funk Exercises

Beginner to Advanced

3.6 - Funk Exercises

17

18

3 3

19

20

3

2/2

3.7 - Funk Grooves

Page Instructions

The grooves on this page are intended for all ranges of students from beginner to advanced. Although, the instructor (or the student) will have a better say at this point as to which part will properly push the student's limits.

For instance, I've had 11-year old beginner students tackle the "50 Ways" groove without issue, and intermediate 17-year old students struggle with "Super Bad." At this stage it is difficult to say. You have likely been at this curriculum for nearly a year in any case. Everyone is different. Just remember to challenge yourself by finding the things you are weakest at and working hardest at those.

The tempos listed are the original tempos of the song. So, playing "I Got the Feeling" at 129 is an advanced challenge, but playing it at 80bpm might be intermediate. Wherever the sticking is important, it is written down for you. Most manuals miss the proper way to play both the "Oakland Stroke" and "50 Ways." But these came straight from the source: Garibaldi and Gadd, respectively. Be certain if you attempt them that you spend a lot of time on the details and the dynamics.

IF YOU ARE A BEGINNER, unless otherwise instructed, please only learn the beginner material. When you finish this curriculum, you will be instructed to return to these pages and review the intermediate material.

Weekly Assignment week #1 (Beginner)

- **Rhythms:** Learn the following with confidence. Memorization is important, but don't expect to remember these forever.
    - Boogaloo Down Broadway
    - Soul Power
    - You're a Sweet, Sweet Man

- Song: *Play That Funky Music Whiteboy* – This is your first exercise in learning funk music. Go to any place on the world-wide web and listen to the song. Notice how tightly played everything is played? Hear the hi-hat openings? Do you catch how the fills are simple, concise and not over-played? What you cannot hear, however, is that he is doing what is called, "burying the beater" in regard to the kick drum. In funk you will be playing the kick pedal so that the beater remains on the kick drumhead *after* the strike. This dampens the sound coming from the kick and creates a more solid impact all at once. Try this technique throughout this song. It may take some getting used to if you have not already been playing the kick drum this way. Learn the groove exactly as written, including the fills, up through the Pre-Chorus. Stop at the Chorus.

Weekly Assignment week #2 (Intermediate)

- **Rhythms:** Learn the following – again, be able to perform them without aid of the material.
    - The Payback
    - Pungee
    - Sissy Strut – Use the exact sticking written. Also, although it is not written here, this is a *half-shuffle* or New Orleans Second-line shuffle or *lazy* shuffle. That means that it is somewhere between a fully tripletized feel and a straight groove. Zigaboo (Joseph) Modeliste popularized (though did *not* invent) that feel. It is impossible to write it down because it is not fully tripletized. If you cannot tell if it is a shuffle or a straight beat ... then it is a New Orleans Second-line feel. It's strictly non-mathematical and inexact, and ALL feel. If you can't feel the half-shuffle, you can't play it.

- **Song**: *Play That Funky Music Whiteboy* – Learn the Chorus section. Notice I wrote, "fill" at the top of the last measure. That means begin using your own fills. But keep in mind that they must be simple. It is important at this stage for you to begin using your own fills to the best of your ability. The rest of the song is up to you to finish at your leisure, as it is mostly the same material played over and over again. Begin learning to read the "road signs" to know where to go (repeats, Da Segno, Coda, et cetera).

3.7 - Funk Grooves

Beginner to Advanced

♩ = 130

♩ = 104

Boogaloo Down Broadway

Soul Power

f

♩ = 110

You're A Sweet, Sweet Man

♩ = 127

Super Bad

♩ = 99

The Payback

l r l l r

♩ = 82

Pungee - The Meters (Zigaboo)

♩ = 88

Sissy Strut - The Meters (Zigaboo)

♩ = 129

I Got The Feeling - James Brown

♩ = 156

Oakland Stroke - Tower of Power (Garibaldi)

3.7 - Funk Grooves

2/2

January 2015, Tracking Lullaby of Birdland at AIMM

Level Four: Intermediate (orange belt) Getting More Complex

4.1 - Dotted 8ths

Page Instructions

You have been dabbling in intermediate material up to this stage. Now you are officially into the intermediate phase of your learning (relative to this curriculum). Prepare to learn how to learn. I have been, since Week One, trying to teach you how to teach yourself. Could that work me out of a job? Not really. There is so very much more beyond this curriculum that you don't yet know what you do not yet know.

In this set of assignments you will begin learning the basic techniques of playing 3's, 5's and 7's within a 4/4 construct. The first three assignments are in dotted 8ths (3's) and will prepare you for the upcoming song material. Notice that the fourth measure of the dotted 8ths exercise is the same as the first. The math is really simple: 16x8 = 8x16. there are 16 dotted 8th notes in three measures; there are eight 16th notes in each measure. So, it only requires three measures to come back around. However you choose to look at it, you will see how the last measure works out to the same as the first. The same math works for 5's and 7's within 16th notes in 4/4 measures.

Weekly Assignment week #1

- **Exercises:** Start learning the first two lines. Take … these … slowly. What method do I continually stress when learning difficult things? Right … one beat at a time, muscle-memory. It is quite tempting to want to immediately push the envelope and play fast. But, just as a reminder, that **will** slow down the learning process. The more mistakes you make, the more often you will make those same mistakes. Muscle memory works both ways. It will remember what you did right, and what you did wrong. Find yourself beating your head against a wall or chewing on your sticks like a rabid bunny? Check your process. I am telling you factually, with a guarantee, that if you follow the muscle memory technique you will get this quickly.

Weekly Assignment week #2

- **Exercises:** Begin learning the third line, "Dotted 8ths" *one measure at a time!* You will need to be able to perform any of these measures individually (and altogether), on call, on demand, starting at any place in the first three measures – and you will need to pull it from your head like a primary language … and still know where you are in a song. I highly recommend that you spend hours at a time on these until you get the feel for them. In an advanced stage they will not be played the way you see them. And you will use them often. I simply cannot stress enough how important these will be to you in the future.
- **Song**: *Bring Me To Life* – Learn just the first verse. You *will need to count* to know when to start playing. Look for the road signs – notice the 2/4 bar after the first verse.

Weekly Assignment week #3

- **Exercises:** "7's in 4/4" – Now that you (hopefully) have absolutely mastered the dotted eights (maybe?), I'm absolutely going to force you into learning 5's and 7's within 4/4. All that means is, in this case, we are counting every fifth, or every seventh, 16th note. This is important for the intermediate skills, but you will likely use it only as often as you creatively choose to. Do your best with it. Try to get the feel for it. That's what is important right now (that means eyes closed!).
- **Song**: *Bring Me To Life* – Chorus 1, Verse 2, Chorus 2.
- Notice the ride cymbal note alternates between a crash-ride and a regular ride (not the bell, please). That means to crash the quarter notes using the blunt of your stick on the edge of the ride cymbal,

followed by more of a tip hit on the fat portion of the cymbal. The thinner cymbals definitely sound better for this job. Talk to your instructor about how to manage this technique.

Weekly Assignment week #4

- **Exercises:** "5's in 4/4" – As painful as this segment has been (drudgery for some, fun for others!), keep with it. It will pay off. You need to be able to perform at least some of this without aid of the material.

- **Song**: *Bring Me To Life* – Instrumental & Bridge. The first two verses of the Instrumental section differ from the 2nd two (which are the same as the verse!); there is a repeat and alternate ending. There are accents above the quarter notes in alternate ending #2. The Bridge is mostly in "cut time," meaning "cut in half" so that the snare lands on "3" instead of "2 & 4." Watch the stop on the last measure of the Bridge section. You can play the rest of the song already.

4.1 - Dotted 8ths and odd time sycopation

Beginner thru Intermediate

♩ = 90

With 8th note HH

DBLS PRACTICE (RIGHT FOOT)

ff

With quarter note HH

DOTTED 8THS (3'S IN 4/4)

SAME AS 1st MEASURE!

7'S IN 4/4

5'S IN 4/4

4.2 - Odd Meter Rhythms

Page Instructions

Odd Meter Rhythms come before Odd Meter Exercises to help you develop the **feel first**. I have included how to count these rhythms, but you may want to substitute your own counting. For instance, the 13/8 rhythm (as divided on the page) could be counted 4+4+5 (=13). Or, you *could* count it 1,2,3,4; 1,2,3,4; 1&2&3&4,5& - OR – you could count it another way – 4+4+4+1, perhaps? But I highly advise *not* counting from 1 to 13. That is just a mouthful and doesn't feel right. You will see that I wrote down how to count the 11/8 rhythm. It is called "odd time" because it is an odd number (not an even number). It does not mean "rare" or "different" but "non-even."

This lesson is all about learning musical subdivision. Subdividing is how you split up a particular count. I have labeled some of these as beginner. I would still advise learning them. The rhythms are all based on the first 3/4 time signature, and build outward from there, adding notes on as you go. Simply count through the 3/4 time, then move to the next one and play the extra notes added to the 3/4 measure. You just played the same thing twice, only with a few extra notes. You need to get the feel for these. And you **do** need to understand how to play them without aid of written material. You don't need to necessarily memorize them. Just learn how they each *feel* by counting through them and subdividing as you see fit.

As an Intermediate student, unless otherwise instructed, please only learn the intermediate material. When you finish this curriculum, you will be instructed to return to these pages and review the advanced material.

Weekly Assignment week #1

- Quarter notes: Get used to how this feels, and make **no assumptions**. Read carefully and count each quarter note with a number. The "&" is reserved for eighths notes. This is not a coordination challenge, but will help your "feel" while either counting or not counting.

Figure 37

- Rudiment: Flam Accent – (figure 37) The Flam Accent and Swiss Army Triplet (next week) are very similar. They sound the same, but are played different. One is based on a single-stroke roll, the other on an inverted double-stroke roll. Both are used differently on the drumkit.

As you can see in the illustration, the flam accent is based on a single-stroke roll "r L R L." By now, you understand the flam, which you learned in 2.1. Start by bringing down both sticks into a LH flam, as written in the illustration. Follow it with RH then LH and repeat. Notice that you just played rLRL, with the first strike being nearly silent. That is the basis of this rudiment.

Weekly Assignment week #2

- Eight notes: The count changes a bit so that you now count each eight note with a number. The "&" is now reserved for sixteenth notes. Notice how this differs from counting quarter notes? Mostly, you'll count these in this manner.

Figure 38

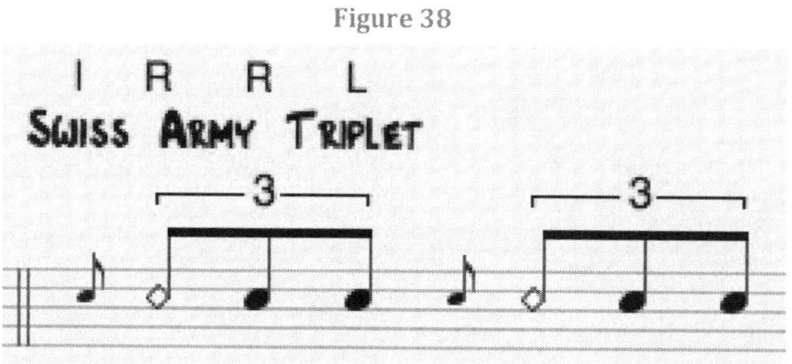

- Rudiment: Swiss Army Triplet – (figure 38) As indicated last week, the Swiss Army Triplet is different from the Flam Accent in only one way – it's based on an inverted double-stroke roll. It can therefore be played as only quickly as you can play an inverted double-stroke roll, which is played as "LRRL" or "RLLR." If you play an inverted double-stroke long enough, eventually you can combine the first and second note into a flam, and you'll have a Swiss Army Triplet. Or you can just learn it slowly, one beat at a time. One method works for some students, the other method works for other students. Try both.

Weekly Assignment week #3

- Sixteenth notes: Notice how the count has shifted to all numbers on 16th notes? Except for 10/16 (which technically is not an 'odd' number but included because it contains two 5/8 counts), which I suggested counting differently. There are no rules at this stage regarding counting. Count it however it best works for you.

- Rudiments: Both Swiss Army and Flam Accent – Begin switching directions, starting with the other stick/hand. And learn to switch between both these rudiments. It will become important to you in future lessons. **If you have any intentions on playing in high school band**, you'll need to know every rudiment I've assigned you so far, and you'll need to know them very well. Otherwise, you'll need them in your drumming anyhow. These are standard requirements in nearly every form of drumming.

4.2 - Odd Meter Rhythms

Beginner thru Advanced

♩ = 120

1 2 & 3 1 2 & 3 4 5 &

QUARTER NOTES (BEGINNER)

EIGHT NOTES (INTERMEDIATE)

(1 2 3 4) (1 2 3 4) (1 2 3)

1 2 & 3 & 4 & 5 &

♩= 90

SIXTEENTH NOTES (ADVANCED)

4.2 - Odd Meter Rhythms

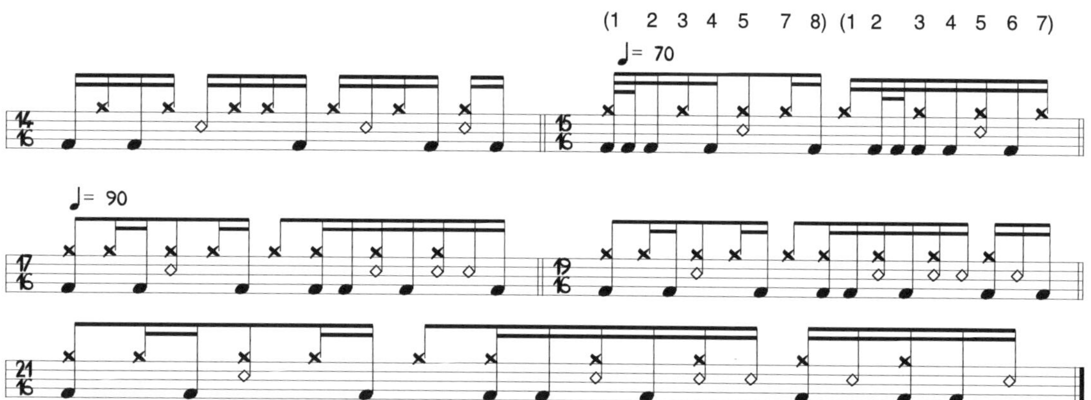

2/2

4.3 - Odd Meter Exercises

Page Instructions

This is where the "homework" begins. On the next page, each line contains: 1) a basic example; 2) the same basic example plus *empty* beats containing only hi-hat notes. Your job is to invent the rest of the rhythm after playing the basic example. All of these are counted in quarter notes. This really should not take too long. Some of these are harder than others, but I have full confidence that you can handle at least most of them at this stage. The purpose of this exercise is to begin learning dictation (the ability to write out a rhythm as you hear it), and to understand odd meter just a little more before we move on.

Fill in your parts – just random kick and snare – beginning where the arrow points downward ("fill in the rest here"), on that exact beat. The intent is to teach you some music *writing* skills. Up to now you have only been taught to *read* the language of music. Today is your first baby step toward being able to write it! And you will find that one skill does not translate into the other very well. You need both skills as a musician. Think of music as any written language. It's easy to learn to speak a language when everyone around you is speaking it. But learning to read and write the language takes *a lot more time* and a totally different skillset.

> **"Aphasias" is when a person can read but not write, or write but not read. It is a disorder. You don't want this disorder in music! Of course, when a person can speak a language but cannot read or write it then that is called *illiterate*. That is a dysfunction. You don't want this dysfunction in music either!**

The pattern in this material is a measure in 3/4 then 5/4 – And then 3/4 then 7/4. So, exercises 1 & 2 are part of the same section.

Weekly Assignment week #1

- **Exercises:** #1 thru #8 – you are not expected to memorize anything. Just write and rehearse, write and rehearse, all the way down.
- **Song**: *Schism* – Only the first Instrumental and Verse sections (which are mostly the same). Do you notice how the metronome is set? ♪= 213

The tempo is 213 but it is set to an eighth note count! Be sure to set your metronome accordingly. The point of learning this section of Schism is to exercise your new odd-meter skills on a very well written drum part. Take note of the places where the hi-hat foot closes the opened hi-hat.

WARNING: this song may intimidate you. But the part I'm asking you to learn is very simple. In fact, you have already done it.

Weekly Assignment week #2

- **Exercises**: #9 thru #18 – by now you have the hang of it. Keep up through the end. There are some rough spots to look for such as #10 (samba) and the #12 Linear Songo. If you have some trouble with any of these, simply do your best to work through them – one beat at a time. You will use these skills upcoming in the curriculum.
- **Song**: *Schism* – keep working on it until it is comfortable. If you have a double-kick pedal, you should go ahead and try to work out how to get those last notes in that second Verse section (last measure before Interlude). You instructor can guide you in this if you are interested.

4.3 - Odd Meter Exercises

5 & 7 alternating

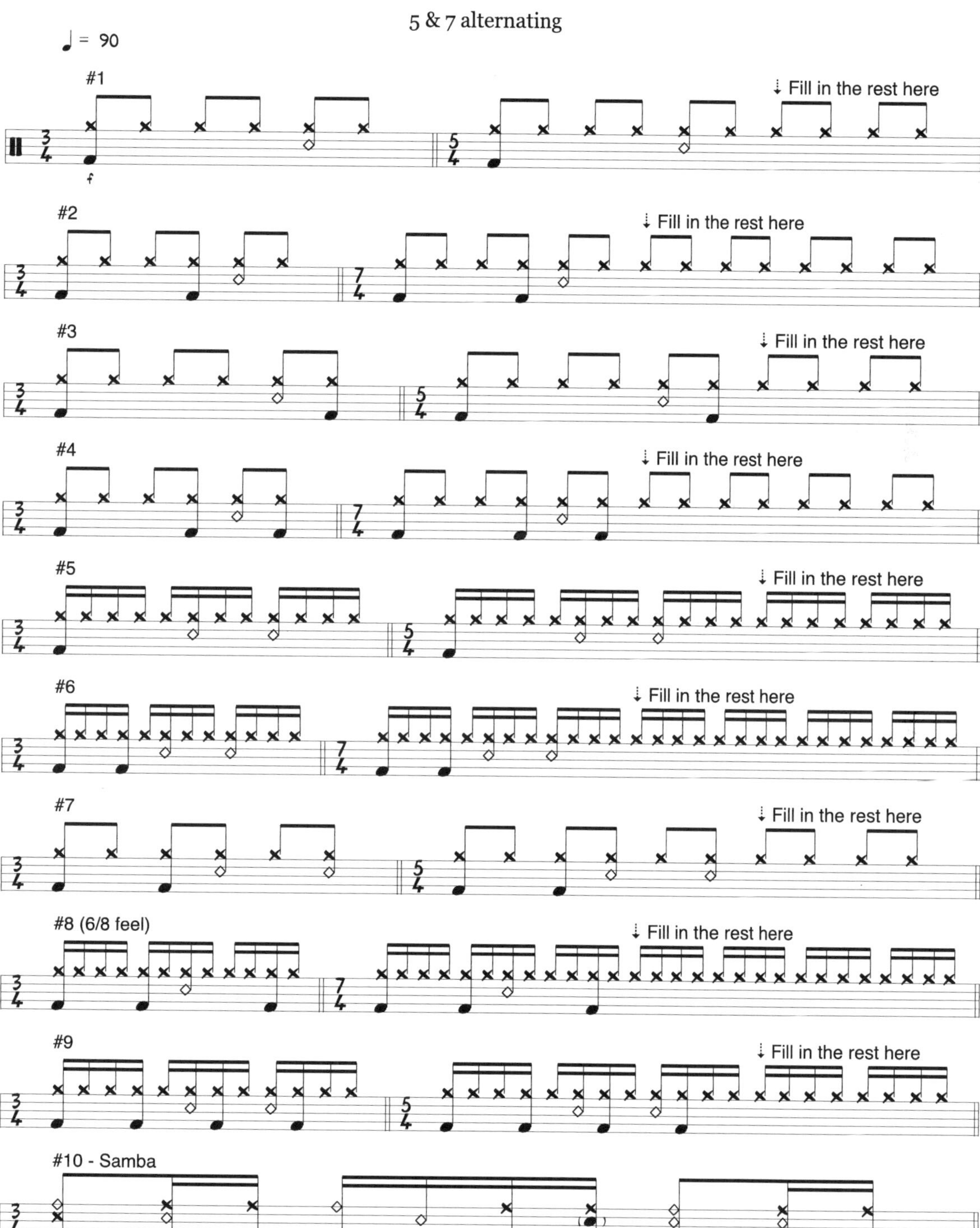

4.3 - Odd Meter Exercises

2/2

4.4 - Linear exercises

Page Instructions

Something new! In drumming, the word, "linear" means that there is only one note per beat – a snare or hi-hat or kick (et cetera) – and no two notes are ever played together. It is linear (one-dimensional) because it is not planar (two-dimensional). The only exception to that rule is if there is an open hi-hat … it needs to close eventually. Therefore, in that case, the hi-hat would close with another voice (part of the instrument) as in exercise C1.

Per the legend at the top of the page, all of the "A" exercises begin with the right foot (RF); all the "B" exercises begin with the LH, and so on. The objective is **to repeat each measure**, not play continually through. And once you have conquered two measures, combine them. Then learn two more; combine them. You will find that some are more difficult. Focus on those.

Watch for accented notes. These create a "pulse" for each rhythm. They will otherwise sound stale and lifeless. Any machine can play a rhythm. Try to offer more than a machine can. All except the last four are in triplet form.

You'll be on these for a while, so try and beat the clock. If you can learn two weeks of material in one week, you can get ahead! **Use a metronome** after you have built up the coordination for any of these measures.

Weekly Assignment week #1

- Rudiment: The Flam Tap – (figure 39) As with the Swiss Army Triplet (why was this not named "inverted flam accent?") and the Flam Accent, the only difference between the Flam Tap and the Inverted Flam tap is that one is based on a single-stroke roll and the other is not. The Flam Tap is based on an inverted triple-stroke roll. A triple stroke-roll is RrrLll. An inverted triple-stroke roll is RllLrr. There are still three in a row on both sides. So, you can only play this rudiment as fast as you can play a triple-stroke roll. This is a very useful drumkit rudiment if you can master it.

Figure 39

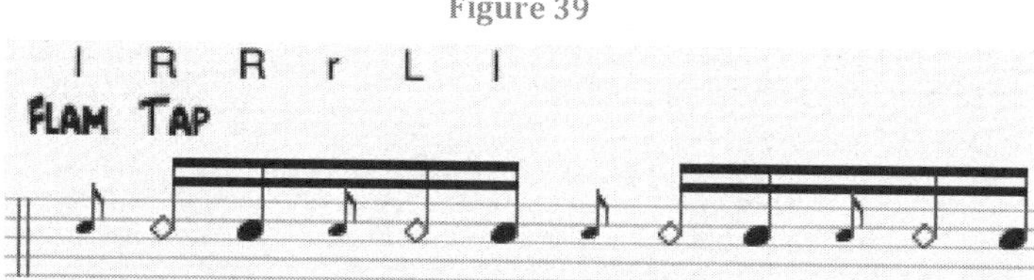

- **Exercises**: A's & B's. Note that B4 has a "quick close." Your instructor may need to demonstrate this. But the idea is to close with LF so quickly that the RH cannot create an open hi-hat sound (the opposite is true for D6-D9).

Weekly Assignment week #2

- Rudiment: The Inverted Flam Tap – (Figure 40) Based on the single-stroke triplet, this is another highly useful drumkit rudiment. Begin by playing RLR(rest)LRL(rest). Then start to flam the first two notes each time. rL-R(rest)lR-L(rest). Then smooth out the strikes so that each strike is evenly played as written in the diagram.

Figure 40

- **Exercises**: C's only. You should have already gone beyond the point where you begin feeling comfortable with these. Hopefully, you have been able to get ahead a little.

Weekly Assignment week #3

- Continue learning both Flam Taps – learn to switch back and forth between them on your practice pad. When you are ready, we'll move it to the drumkit to experiment.

- **Exercises**: D's only. It will feel a little awkward at first because these are not in triplet form.

At this point, begin combining any of these measures together, including tripletized and non-tripletized (together) if you choose. Report back to your instructor with your inventions.

4.4 - Linear Exercises

A=RF; B=LH; C=RH; D=LF

Moderate ♩ = 140

A1 A2 A3 A4

ff

A5 B1 B2 B3

B4 Quick close B5 B6 B7

C1 C2 C3 C4

C5 C6 C7 r l C8

C9 D1 D2 D3

D4 D5 D6

D7 D8 r l D9

4.5 - Triples, Quads, Quints

Page Instructions

"Triple … quadruple … quintuple" is the basis of this lesson. You will not get into the quintuples yet. That is for an advanced phase. The idea of "gospel chops" originates here. You will need to learn these carefully and slowly. Remember that the hi-hat foot *must keep the time*. Otherwise, you, the listeners and other musicians may not know what you're doing or where you are in the ideas. As you get faster and faster with these exercises you will find greater and greater uses for them. **These are required** in order to enter the advanced phase of this curriculum.

> Remember, *it's easy to go easy on yourself*. Pushing yourself is always difficult, but it always pays off in high dividends. **Use a single kick pedal**, not a double, for these exercises.

Although this is written in all *rimshots*, that is not expected. What is expected is that you begin to "move around the kit" with these exercises, meaning that the hands should be able to freely navigate from a tom, to a cymbal, a ride, hi-hat … at will, without difficulty – while performing each measure. Just replace the snare with whatever you want to hit instead, as you get more proficient at it.

Note: Triples are not "triplets." A "triplet" is a rudiment that is played: RlrLrl. Triples differ from this because it is a linear exercise and is not a rudiment.

Weekly Assignment week #1

Figure 41

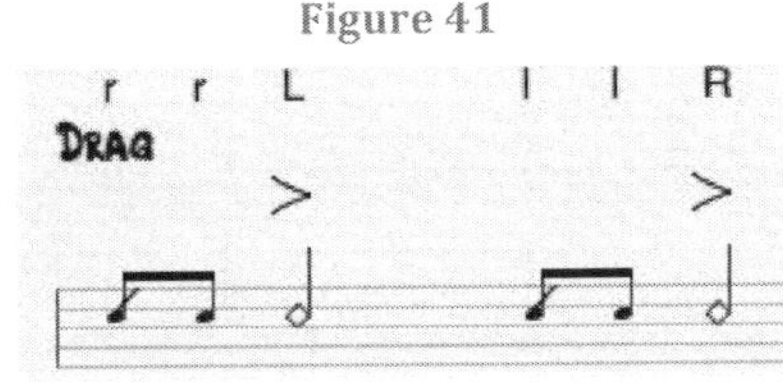

- Rudiment: The Drag – (figure 41) You will need to know this rudiment for the song you will be learning over the next three or four weeks. Use the double-stroke **bounce** technique to accomplish the first two notes. It's a simple rudiment. The first two notes are NOT played as sixteenth notes. This rudiment is called a "drag," because the two first notes are played *just before* the accented note. You will need to learn them both directions, as written, although not necessarily together.

- **Exercises**: The first six measures are vital. Be certain to *really know* these exercises. They will serve you well in the near future. In fact, you're going to need them for the assigned song. At this point begin combing them. Move from one measure to the other. The only rule is you cannot have three consecutive kick drum notes. Figure out how these measures can be combined.

- **Song**: *La Grange* – The hoop-rim section at the beginning and middle of this song is simply legendary. Frank Beard (the only one without a beard in the band) created something rather original there. Use the rim of the snare (the hoop) for this. By now you should already know the "drag" rudiment. Learning to shuffle at 159bpm may take some instruction from your teacher. Comfortably playing at that speed requires a good grasp of the **drop/catch** (drop/pull) **technique**. Have your instructor show you how to do this. Meanwhile, use a slow-downer app or software to be able to play along, or just use a metronome. The fill at the end of this section is note-for-note as Beard played it. It is important to get it right so take your time. Use alter**nating** sticking. Pay attention to the rimshots.

Weekly Assignment week #2

- <u>Rudiment</u>: The Flam Drag – (figure 42) as an intermediate player, you're almost finished with the rudiments in this curriculum. A rounded player will know how to perform nearly all of these rudiments on demand, although some of them are not drumkit essentials.

Figure 42

- You already know the "drag" rudiment, as well as the "flam." You may alternate these if you wish, but they are written as a right-handed flam first, then a left-handed, to show you how to play both directions. If you are uncertain of the rhythm, look *only* at the snare accents/rimshots – they are just 8th notes! If you ignore the grace notes and the drag notes then all that remains are 8th notes. It really makes reading easier when you start with the bare notes.

- **Exercises**: Lines 3 & 4. Alternating, double-paradiddle, paradiddle; triples in dotted 8ths. They are not meant to be played together. However, at first learn each individually.

- **Song**: *La Grange* – Instrumental section. As indicated in the transcription, there appears to be some overdubbing here. Either the hi-hat or the snare was overdubbed with the ride cymbal. In any case, use the **ride cymbal** for this part – it is written on the line where the ride cymbal goes, regardless of the shape of the note.

Weekly Assignment week #3

- **Exercises**: Quads! <u>First line only.</u> Learn to combine these measures! Same rule: do not allow three consecutive kick drum notes, because at high speeds that would be quite difficult if not impossible.

- **Song**: *La Grange* – Here's where the payoff begins, if you've been working hard. The fill at the end of the first verse is note-for-note how Beard played it. The difficulty I have found with students is learning how to fit this into a measure properly. If it helps you, try to think of it as a "flam/kick" (x6). This fill forces you to hit the crash with the snare on the first note of the Lead section as written.

  You will begin by playing the following (figure 43) within the same tempo at which you have learned the rest of the song:

43Figure 3

Figure 44

Next, play it this way, still using the metronome (figure 44):

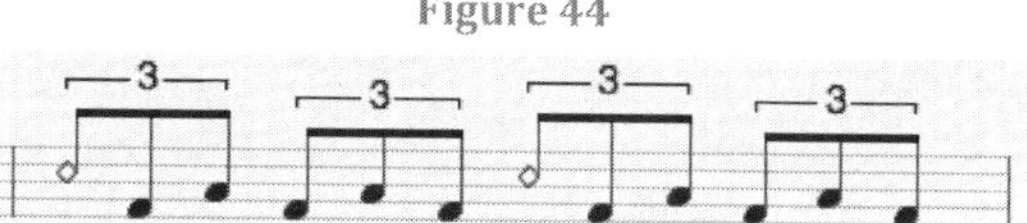

Now you are ready to make those single strikes into flams.

Weekly Assignment week #4

- **Exercises**: Quads: <u>Second line only</u>. This begins your journey into mixing quads into triplets (not trip<u>les</u>). Don't worry if you don't really get this one just yet. In time, with enough work, it will become natural. But you're going to see this again in a later phase of this curriculum. Best to learn the basic idea now.

- **Song**: *La Grange* – Lead 1 and the Bridge. The rest of the song you already know how to play. The bridge is a little awkward unless you ignore the guitar and keep the count going. The guitar is playing in triplet 8th notes. The drummer is not. Choke the first cymbal note. See your instructor for how to properly do this without injury. A "choke" is where one hand "chokes" the cymbal before it can ring out after the other stick hits it. Hit the cymbal with one hand (the RH in this case) and choke it with the other (LH).

4.5 - Triples, Quads, Quints

♩ = 80

1 & 2 &

Triples

Alternating

Double-paradiddle in triplet form

Paradiddle in triplet form

Triples played in dotted 8th form

r l r l r l r l l r l r r l r l

Quads

r l r l r l r l r l r l l r l r l r r l r l

Quads in Triplet form

r l r l r l

Quints (advanced)

Ride fill using quints

4.6A – Music Styles

Page Instructions

This is your first introduction to various styles of drumming. So far, you have learned some funk, rock, blues and jazz. This first page covers some of the basics of most styles.

Listen to the following songs to get familiar with some of these rhythms:

- *Rosanna* by Toto
- *Three Little Birds* by Bob Marley
- *Working Man Blues* by Merle Haggard
- *Poor Tom* by Led Zeppelin (Coda)
- *Sissy Strutt* by The Meters
- *Satch Boogie* by Joe Satriani
- *Hot For Teacher* by Van Halen
- *Cold Shot* by Stevie Ray Vaughn

Weekly Assignment week #1

- **Rhythms:** *#1 - #7*
    - Rhythm #1 is a simplified version of a funk shuffle. For simplification, it does not contain the ghost notes commonly played in this rhythm.
    - Rhythm #2 and #3 are the exact same rhythm. One is straight 16ths and the other is played as a shuffle (or swing) feel. Learn how to switch back and forth this week. Next week you'll learn more on how to do this.
    - Rhythm #4 and #5 are very similar. Both are a "half-swing" or "lazy shuffle" feel. The first, New Orleans Second Line, is played exactly as written. The feel is somewhere between straight and swing! This is very important to understand. Please ask your instructor to demonstrate this technique. It cannot be written out. If music uses whole numbers then the half-swing is a decimal point! You can shift it anywhere between a straight and swing/shuffle, depending upon the feel of the music. John Bonham (Led Zeppelin) was known for his swing feel.
    - The challenge for #6 is to keep the 16th notes clean! If you are uncertain, try leading with your LF and listen – somehow this helps to hear inconsistencies.
    - The challenge for #7 is to decide whether to lead with your LF or RF. Whichever you decide, stick with it. Keep it clean – no flams between the snare and kick drum.

Weekly Assignment week #2

- **Rhythms**: *#8 thru #12*
    - Rhythm #8 – here you will further experiment in shifting a rhythm from straight to swing and back again. Just count the quarter notes, and consult your instructor if you have any doubts at all.
    - Rhythm #9 may seem simple. We have yet to discuss "pocket" because it's more of an advanced concept. Just know that where the 2&4 (or the 4&10) snare strikes is often somewhere microscopically behind or ahead of the beat. In this case, it is going to be behind the metronome click. Again, this is more of an advanced concept. Just be mindful of it for now. The trick here is to relax your grip, loosen the stick in your hand, raise the swing of the stick, and even your whole arm, and cause a slower groove. Your instructor will be glad to assist, I'm certain, if you have any difficulty or doubts.
    - #10 is played with RH only on hi-hat – no alternating stick patterns.

- #11 is a **tight shuffle**. That means – again – the beat of "a/uh" is somewhere between a normal shuffle and a 16th note. Listen to Cold Shot for a good example.
- #12 is the same rhythm is Blue Jeans Blues (ZZ Top) that you worked on in lesson 2.2, with the small addition of the "a/uh" snare hit before the beat of "3." You can also count this rhythm in 12/8, if you prefer.

4.6a - Music Styles

♩ = 73

♩ = 75 ♩ = 75

1 - Funk Shuffle 2 - Reggae (straight) 3 - Reggae (swing)

♩ = 100 ♩ = 140

4 - New orleans Second Line (Lazy shuffle) 5 - Train (Country and Western)

♩ = 120 ♩ = 250

6 - Dbl-kick rock 7 - Dbl-kick rock shuffle

Shift #8 from straight to swing!

♩ = 115

8 - 1/2 time funk

♩ = 60 ♩ = 90

9 - 12/8 ballad 10 - R&B

♩ = 140 ♩ = 80

11 - Tight Texas swing 12 - Blues shuffle

4.6B – MUSIC STYLES - LATIN

Page Instructions

In the following styles assignment, you will be taught the very basics of Latin rhythms, which are *often* named for the dance that may accompany a rhythm, not for the rhythm itself or anything musical. For instance, the *bossa* and the *samba* are exactly the same rhythm played at different speeds in the way that a 4/4 rock beat and ballad are the exact same rhythm at different speeds. The bossa is a slower dance than the samba. The cascara is played in salsa dances during the verses and during softer sections.

A *clave* (klä-vā) is how we describe the patterns played (often using the LH) on whatever voice on the drumset or whatever instrument, but is derived from the clave *instrument*, which is two cylindrical sticks that are clicked together. There is no one particular clave rhythm. A *son* (pronounced "sŌn") clave is slightly different than a *rhumba* clave. There are two basic types of clave rhythms: a 2:3 and 3:2. That is not a ratio. That is a way to describe how the first part of rhythm is played against the second part of the rhythm. In a 2:3 clave there are two clave beats played in the first half, and three in the second half, as you will see in the following page.

Also, bear in mind that *most often Lain rhythms are written over two 2/4 measures.* It can be frustrating to read it that way. However, it is the historical way to read Latin percussion. As a comparison, let's use illustrate using the Tumbao:

The standard (legacy) way it is written:

1 & a 2 & 1 & a 2 &

The modern way it is written:

1 & a 2 & 3 & a 4 &

The way it is most easily understood, in 4/4, is NOT how it is written as a standard. Some instructors teach Latin using the 2/4 historically accurate method. Most modern books today use 4/4 as a standard to teach Latin. As a result, I will include both in this book.

Weekly Assignment week #1

- **Rhythms:** *The Tumbao, Songo and Samba* – These are the basic rhythms using only 8th note hi-hat ostinatos, with only the kick drum. You will need to learn these three basic constructs and remember them. You'll need to know them well enough to recall them at any time. Note the kick drum ghost notes followed by accents on the samba.

- **Rhythms:** *All basic four claves* – Again there is no kick drum. These are basic constructs for you to know, remember and recall. You'll need to be able to verbally and rhythmically differentiate between all four.

Weekly Assignment week #2

- **Rhythms:** *The Mozambique* – basic construct. You're about to embark on combining all of these ideas. When you get to section lesson 5.1 you're really going to rely upon knowing all these basic constructs inside and out. For now, learn just these rhythms (well enough to be able to play on demand), and count it aloud: 1-&- 2e-a -e&- 4e-a
    - Add the samba kick to the Mozambique, as well as accenting the ride cymbal in certain places. At first this will seem uncomfortable. But if you continue to work hard, it will go by quickly and you'll get it.

Weekly Assignment week #3

- **Rhythms***: Mozambique (Steve Gadd Style)* – Drumming legend, Steve Gadd, developed a unique way to play both a Mozambique and a tumbao rhythm at the same time. It is almost a linear except for the first note. Try it first with kick drum, then replace kick drum with RH.
    - Use the LH on the hi-hat, RH on snare – Play it open-handed.
    - Now move around the kit using this idea. Use the toms instead of the snare.
    - Add the samba kick drum rhythm to this pattern. Now you can see how many different combinations you might come up with on your own!
- **Rhythms:** *Bossa/Samba* rhythms – All of them. This is where you combine a samba/bossa with a clave pattern. There are no accents. Just learn them as they are.

Drummer Listening Recommendations

Start listening to some drummers such as: *Art Blakey, Benny Greb, Bernard Purdie, Billy Higgins, Billy Cobham, Buddy Rich, Butch Miles, Carter Beauford, Chris Coleman, Dave Weckl, David Garibaldi, Dennis Chambers, Dom Famularo, Gary Novak, Gene Krupa, Horacio Hernandez, Jeff Porcarro, Jeff Sipe, Joe Morello, John Blackwell, John Bonham , Jo (papa) Jones, Joe (philly) Jones, JoJo Mayer, Keith Carlock, Louis Bellson, Marco Minnemann, Max Roach, Neil Peart, Peter Erskine, Simon Phillips, Steve Gadd, Steve Smith, Stewart Copeland, Todd Sucherman, Tony Royster Jr, Tony Williams Vinnie Colaiuta Virgil Donati.*

You can learn from any drummer, good or bad. But start with the "greats." Get them in your head. Get obsessed.

4.6b - Music Styles - Latin

♩ = 90

1 a & 3 a &

Tumbao

Songo

Samba

2:3 Son Clave

2:3 Rhumba Clave

3:2 Son Clave

3:2 Rhumba Clave

1 & 2 e a e & 4 e a

Mozambique (basic)

With Samba and bell accents

Can be stick or kickdrum

Mozambique (Steve Gadd Style)

With samba kick and tumbao toms

Bossa/Samba 2:3 Son

Bossa/Samba 2:3 Rhumba

Bossa/Samba 3:2 Son

Bossa/Samba 3:2 Rhumba

4.6b - Music Styles - Latin

in standard 2/4

♩ = 90

1 a & 1 a &

Tumbao

f

Songo

Samba

2:3 Son Clave

f

2:3 Rhumba Clave

f

3:2 Son Clave

f

3:2 Rhumba Clave

f

1 & 2 e a e & 2 e a

Mozambique (basic)

f

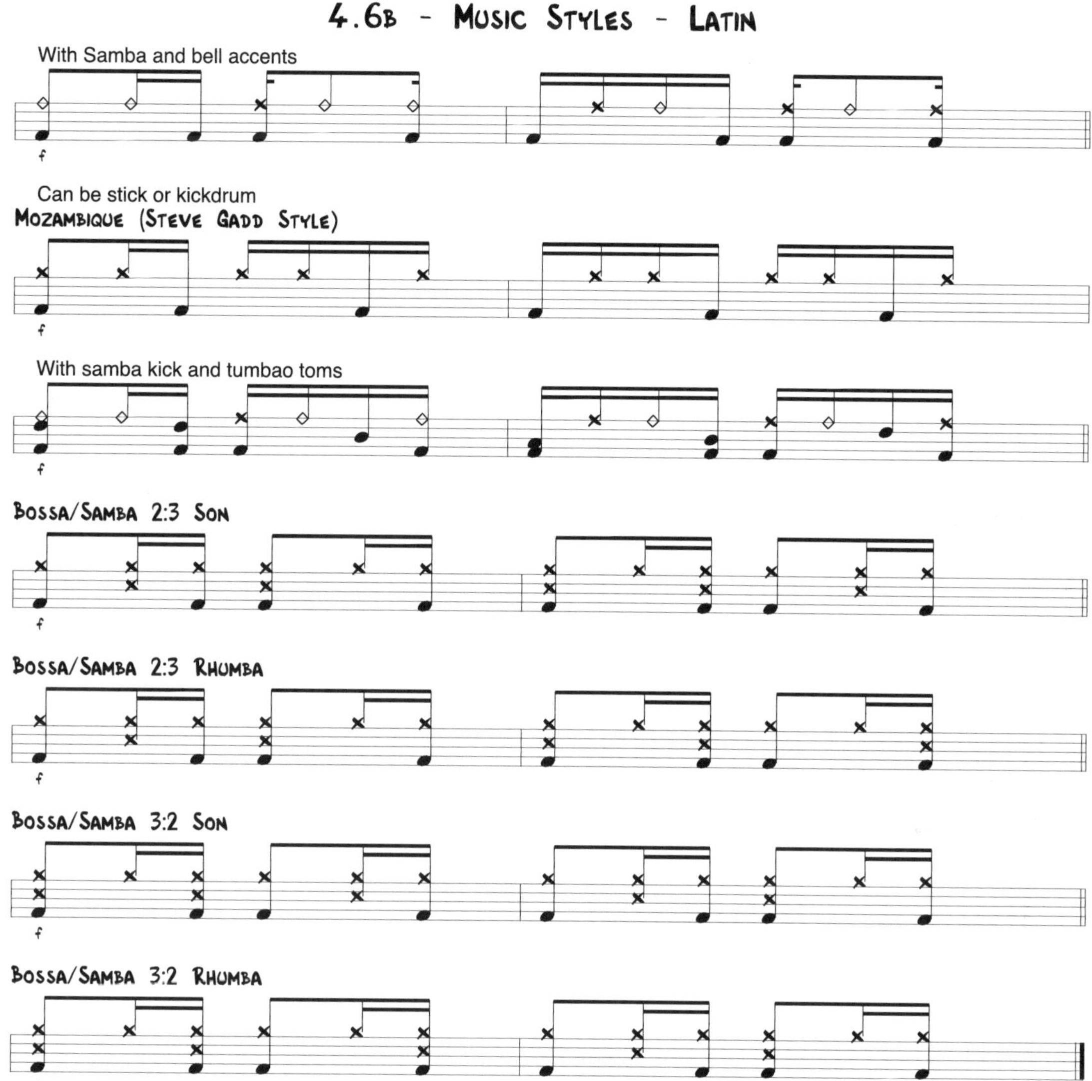
4.6B - Music Styles - Latin
With Samba and bell accents
f
Can be stick or kickdrum
Mozambique (Steve Gadd Style)
f
With samba kick and tumbao toms
f
Bossa/Samba 2:3 Son
f
Bossa/Samba 2:3 Rhumba
f
Bossa/Samba 3:2 Son
f
Bossa/Samba 3:2 Rhumba
f

2/2

4.7 - Kick Drum Reading Exercise #2 (16th Notes)

Page Instructions

The instructions are the same as in 2.7. Only now, you are working with 16th notes. This exercise will assist you in learning to recognize patterns faster. The idea is to play straight through without stopping. Take it slow at first.

While at home write out the count above each note (in pencil to allow for mistakes) just as I did for you on the first line. The reason they are not pre-written on all the measures is because that is for *you to learn* how to do. Have your instructor check your work for you. Count aloud during practice until you grow accustomed to the patterns.

Pick one of the rhythms at the bottom of the page that does **not** have a kick drum pattern. Apply that rhythm to this page starting at line #1.

Remember to use this formula:

1) Kick drum only
2) RH + RF
3) LH + RF
4) LF + RF
5) RH + LH
6) RH + LF
7) LH + LF
8) ALL together

After you have conquered one pattern from the bottom of the page, on your own time come back and learn another one. This is a coordination building challenge as well as a sight-reading builder.

Weekly Assignment week #1

- Learn everything up until the "segno" 𝄋 symbol. Remember to recognize "both, left, right" regarding foot patterns. Start with just the feet: Both, right, left … whatever the pattern is.

Weekly Assignment week #2

- Continue from Segno until "Da Coda." Remember to obey the road signs (repeats, segno, coda).

Weekly Assignment week #3

- Learn from the "Da Coda" to the end. By the end of this week you should be burned out on this exercise but your reading skills will be exponentially greater. You are ready for the next phase of this curriculum.

Remember Why You're Doing This

Take some time out for yourself on the drumkit while you are learning this curriculum. Have fun. Do some click training. Learn a song that pushes your limits. Watch a video by one of your favorite drummers and try to figure out what s/he's doing. Get out and drum. Volunteer to drum at your local church/synagogue. Get some friends together and garage-band it out. Remember why you began to train: to have fun and be good at it.

4.7 - Kick Drum Reading Exercise #2

16th notes
(Play Straight Through)

♩ = 72

1 2 3 4 & a 1 e & 2 & a 3 a 4 a 1 a 2 & e 4 a

Da Coda

D.S. al Coda

#1 #2 #3 #4

RHYTHMS (SNARE, RIDE, HH)

July 24, 2014 - North Georgia Fair Grounds, Anderson Music Hall, Hiawassee, GA (opening for Joe Diffie)

LEVEL FIVE: HIGHER INTERMEDIATE (GREEN BELT) EXPANDING YOUR DRUMMING

5.1 - Linear Fills and Rhythms

Page Instructions

You have reached the intermediate phase of this curriculum. If you worked hard up to this point, then **you should be ready for this material**. *If you find that you are having more difficulty than expected*, or if this seems like its too much, then you'll need to go back and work on the previous material until you feel comfortable with this section. Don't be discouraged in any case. Your instructor will know if you are ready to move into this section, and you should feel confident in doing so. However, if you reviewed this section already then you will immediately notice two things: 1) there isn't as much material to work on; 2) it's all much harder! That is because you are ready for it. Be prepared to spend much more time with each page, more detailed study time and more heavy lifting on your part.

When it comes to linears creativity is important, but so is influence. What rhythms most influence you will be the biggest part of the melting pot from which you derive your own ideas. This lesson is intended to help you sort out a few possibilities. Some of these are my own ideas. Some are standard and used globally and therefore have no main author. Some are iconic to certain artists and attributed to them. Be sure to learn them *up to the assigned tempos*. But start slowly.

Weekly Assignment week #1

- Rudiment: The Buzz Roll also called the Multiple Bounce Roll. Though not technically a rudiment, it is a fundamental skill and is therefore listed on the Percussive Arts Society main list of rudiments. Creating a "buzz" sound requires a certain push into the stick, using more arm than usual, and the forefinger … essentially breaking all the rules. There really is no easy way to teach this. Every student has difficulty at first trying to create this sound effect on the snare. But here are some basic pointers:
    1. To create the 'buzz,' drop one stick to the head from about two inches high, and then allow it to create multiple bounces. Do it again and cut the sound short using more pressure.
    2. Use the furthest edge of the snare head. The closer to the middle you get, the more defined (and louder) the sound becomes. You want a smooth, blurred buzz from the snare wires.
    3. Don't tighten the snare wires too tight.
    4. Push into the snare during a single-stroke roll, but not so much that it sounds dead.
    5. This is mostly an arm-only technique.
    6. Use your ear. Don't allow any *accents* of any kind. It should sound smooth with no gaps.

- **Rhythms:** The *Rod Morgenstein* (Winger, Dixie Dregs) *linear* was from his instructional video, *Putting It All Together*. He is a left-handed drummer, but this linear is adapted for right-handed players. As with everything else, the sticking is written above each note in the measure. Both measures are identical except for the toms in the second measure. But the sticking remains the same, which makes it an easy linear rhythm. Watch the accents at the end of measure two!
- **Rhythms:** The *Steve Gadd Linear* is all RH on hi-hat and LH on snare. It is an inverted double-stroke rhythm throughout. It is actually played in 4/4. But for readability, it is written in 2/4. Be sure and learn the accents as well. They are an important part of this linear.
- **Rhythms:** *Latinized Linear #1 & #2* – both are similar. If you do not have a cowbell, you may want to run out and get this essential instrument. Mount it where your RH can reach it freely. It will be integral to your sound in the future. Avoid a tiny, or overly large, cowbell. Somewhere in the middle is best. Linear #1 has instructions for a "splashed" hi-hat. Simply tap the hi-hat pedal with your LF and release. This requires breaking the rule of "no

Figure 45

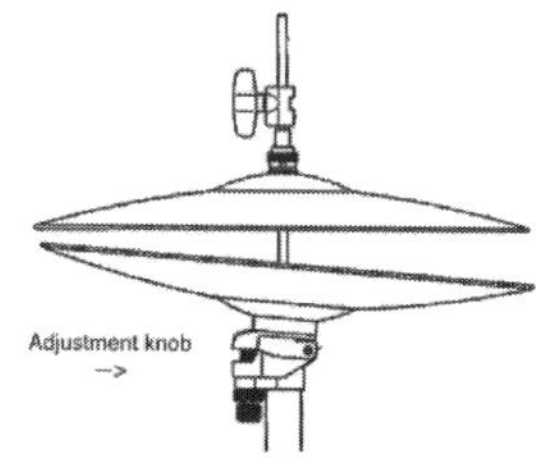

muscles above the knee" for a moment. *You will need to adjust the hi-hat cymbal seat knob* that is below the bottom cymbal so that the bottom cymbal is tilted (figure 45).

- **Rhythms:** *Latinized Linear #3* – Watch where the hi-hat foot lands and follow the sticking written above the measure.
- **Song**: *Losing It* (Rush) – Learn just the first verse section to get the feel of the song. There are three pages. You will assuredly need to count through it if 5/8 or 10/8 are not natural to you. I learned this song in my own intermediate stage, around 1983 (though I may be giving away my age there!).

Weekly Assignment week #2

- **Rhythms:** *Hi-hat Foot Linear* – This is based off the first Gadd linear from last week. There are two measures. The sticking is tricky. The hi-hat foot is integral to the sound. Take this one slow and learn it right.
- **Rhythms:** *Tripletized Quads in 4/4* – As far as coordination is concerned, you can do this. However, the lesson is in the *feel*, which is not what it may seem. Playing quads in triplet form is relatively new for you in this curriculum. If you have any issues with this one, go back to 4.5 and study "Quads in Triplet Form" until you get the feel for it. Then return to this exercise. Use the bell of the ride cymbal where it is indicated and only one rimshot. Remember an 'x' in drum music is not any particular sound. It can be a *foot* hi-hat, a *hand* hi-hat, a cross-stick or a quiet ride cymbal. Remember to look where the note is placed, not just its shape.
- **Song**: *Losing It* (Rush) – Learn the second verse. This is where it becomes more complicated. Note the hi-hat opening at the end of the measure, and that it closes on "1." Also notice that the RH ride part is 'x' meaning "soft" not the bell, and that it is played *with* the crash cymbal (both LH and RH at the same time).

Weekly Assignment week #3

- **Rhythms:** *Linear Pattern #1* – This is quite uncomplicated compared to what you have done thus far. Technically, because of the snare on "4" it is not a linear. But it is close enough.
- **Rhythms:** *Tripletized 2:3 Rhumba & Basic Tripletized 3/4* – both of which were leftover creative inertia from several hours of practice time on my part. Pay close attention to the rimshots and accents.
- **Rhythms:** *Linear Patterns #2 thru #4* are fairly simple. But again, get them in your head.
- **Song**: *Losing It* (Rush) – Bridge, Chorus sections. The Lead is complicated and I'm not expecting you to learn it. But if you are so inclined, please do.

Use this material to create your own rhythms! You should have already had many ideas coursing through you with all that left over creative energy that this exercise (hopefully) created for you. Use it; write them down. Show them to your instructor.

5.1 - Linear Fills and Rhythms

Advanced

♩ = 160

R L L R L L R L L R L L R L R L L L L L R L L R L L R L

ROD MORGENSTEIN LINEAR

f

R

splashed Hi-Hat

♩= 85

STEVE GADD LINEAR

♩= 115

LATINIZED LINEAR #1

r l l r l r l r l l r l r

♩= 120

LATINIZED LINEAR #2

♩= 100

LATINIZED LINEAR #3

l l r r l l L r r l l r r r l r l l Rr l l R L l l r r l r l r l r l r

♩= 150

BASIC LINEAR

♩= 110

HI-HAT FOOT LINEAR

R R L L

♩= 90

TRIPLETIZED QUADS IN 4/4

♩= 140

LINEAR PATTERN #1

TRIPLETIZED 2:3 RHUMBA

♩= 100

BASIC TRIPLETIZED 3/4

5.1 - Linear Fills and Rhythms

R I

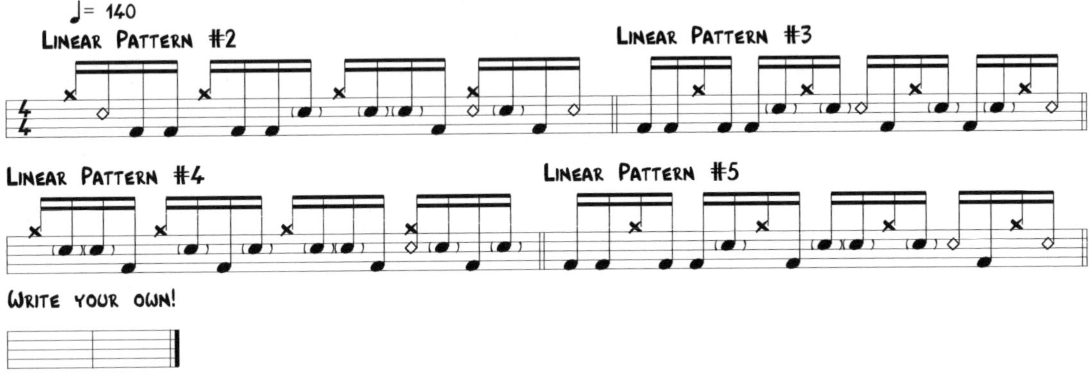

2/2

5.2 - Latin Rhythms – Level 1

Page Instructions

"I'm sick of Latin rhythms! Can we please do something else?" Nope. This will affect your drumming skills for the remainder of your life. I'm going to get on the soapbox and tell you that if you choose to limit your skills to any one genre, or exclude any one genre of music then you will be significantly reducing your ability to market yourself as a drummer, much less a musician. That is the harsh reality. But I'm here to rescue you from this fate. I once had a student tell me that she didn't want to consider how much she could be paid for drumming because it was all about art. Well, the second half is true. It is about art. But artist like to eat, and when they get older they like to feed their children. We can choose to do something else that perhaps we don't like for a living and *not get paid* as a musician, or be a full time musician and get paid for it and do *only that*. If I waved $2,500 at you just to play a simple quarter-note kick drum rhythm for three hours, would you say, "No, I prefer to not get paid?" The skills you get from this section will vastly improve you as a drummer. You may very well astound your peers. Work hard at it; be obsessed until you conquer it.

The last time you explored Latin rhythms was in 4.6b where basic ideas were explained. If you had problems with that assignment, you may want to revisit it. If you are confident enough to push forward then look over this entire assignment first – all the material – and then start at the top. This material differs from the "*4.6b - Music Styles – Latin*" page in that you will now be learning more detailed skills on each of the Latin drumming styles plus some new combinations. There are some more complex concepts in this section and it will take you much more time to learn some of it. Since you have arrived into intermediate drumming, you will be *expected* to observe accents, ghost notes, rimshots, ride-bell and cross-stick notation without assistance. Be certain to closely study what you are learning and assume nothing.

You are going to learn the following Latin rhythms: **bossa, bossa nova, samba, cascara, Mozambique, tumbao and songo**. These rhythms **should take you far longer** to learn than anything you have yet accomplished. But the payoff is tremendous. Look into the drummer, Heracio Hernandez. He is perhaps the most in-demand Cuban/Latin jazz-fusion drummer on the planet at this time. You will find that he keeps a perfect clave going through most of his drum solo work, with his left foot. That is one of the things that make him exceptional.

Again, there are both legacy and modern methods included in this book since both are used still today: 2/4 & 4/4.

Weekly Assignment week #1

- **Rhythms**: *All bossa rhythms* including bossa nova. Be sure to get these up to the recommended speed. These are the easiest of the assignments you will be learning but they are the foundation for what is coming next. Know these rhythms by name. Test yourself. Have someone call one out and you play it. Then play one and name it. You need to know the difference between each concept: 2:3, 3:2, rhumba and son.

Weekly Assignment week #2

- **Rhythms**: *All songo rhythms*. The hi-hat just became much more difficult. The count of the pattern is: 1-&-,2e-a,3-&a,(4)e-a [the "(4)" is not played].

Weekly Assignment week #3

- **Rhythms**: *Samba & both Mozambique rhythms*. You will be expected to pick up the tempo at the end of the week, but for now *play these one beat at a time,* then very slowly. These are suggested ways to learn these rhythms. The possible combinations for any number of them are nearly infinite. Learn to be creative.

- **Rhythms:** The *Mozambique with Tumbao* has a few crucial elements to it:
    - although the ride pattern is simply eighth notes there are bell accents every "#" of the count;
    - the kick drum is a *tumbao* rhythm;
    - the hi-hat foot is always on the "&" of the beat.
    - Learn this rhythm "one beat at a time" in combination with the layering method in Section 1(e) *Steps to Learning Any Rhythm*;
    - the snare is the actual *mozambique* rhythm and is written with an accent on the first beat – however, the objective is to be able to vacillate that accent to *any* beat. So repeat this measure by *displacing* the accent one beat over, each time you play the measure. **The first time**, it will be on "1" then on "e" then on "&" and on "a" and so on.

Weekly Assignment week #4

- **Rhythms**: *All of the 6/8 clave patterns*. The main pattern is played on the cowbell. The first three are standard patterns with the cowbell for americanized Latin music. Amongst many others in this book, the last cowbell pattern is my own and does not come from any other source. Notice that the hi-hat pattern in each is different. These are the four basic ways you *could* play a hi-hat. Don't ever limit yourself – really stretch your own ideas.

Welcome to the painful part!

No pain, no gain, as the axiom goes. You are in the intermediate stage now. Yes, this is difficult and it is going to take you some time. But be patient, learn each rhythm using the "one beat at a time" method, and the layering method (or some combination of the two) from Section 1(e). This will pay off huge for you. **If you cannot force yourself to work this hard**, then you will be resigning to becoming a basic drummer. There is nothing really wrong with that if that is what you want. Plenty of drummers get paid for supplying just a basic beat. However, if you find that you have great ambitions then push yourself. But make up your mind to never sit in the middle. Sitting in the middle will only be painful because from here on out it gets tougher, with or without this curriculum, any instructor or me. But I'm trying to build a fine drummer in you. I am confident you can do it if you apply my steps, and if you really *want* it. Find some influences. Listen to them.

Know Your Instrument

I recommend getting very intimate with your drumkit now. Sit down with it. Take it apart (yes, really!). Find out what makes it tick. Experiment with different tunings (see my reference page on *Basics of Tuning a Drumkit* for more information). Experiment with different drumheads. What works best for your drum configuration? Have you arranged your kit so that it is comfortable? Don't be afraid of taking it apart. It goes right back together. This is a good time to begin learning not to be intimidated by the idea of disassembling your drums. Really, it is absolutely essential that you know how to do so. Most serious musicians know how to do this with their instrument(s). You should too, and drums are certainly no exception to the rule. See Section 1(j), *The Proper Care and Feeding of Your Drumkit.*

5.2 - Latin Rhythms

Level 1

♩ = 60

↓ Son Clave 3:2

↓ Rhumba Clave 3:2

BOSSA

f

↓ Son Clave 2:3

↓ Rhumba Clave 2:3

↓ Ride cymbal

♩= 60

2:3 BOSSA NOVA

↓ Accented ride bell

♩= 95

SAMBA

↓ #1 Cascara songo + 2:3 son

↓ #2 Cascara songo + 2:3 rhumba

↓ #3 Cascara songo + 3:2 rhumba

SONGO

↓ dispursed snare accents

MOZAMBIQUE WITH TUMBAO

↓ Ride = Cascara #2

DISPERSED MOZAMBIQUE

↓ Hi-Hat Variant #1

♩= 110

6/8 STANDARD CLAVE PATTERN

↓ Hi-Hat variant #2

6/8 RHUMBA CLAVE

↓ Hi-Hat Variant #3

6/8 SON CLAVE

↓ Hi-Hat variant #4

6/8 ALTERNATIVE

5.2 - Latin Rhythms

Level 1

5.2 - Latin Rhythms

↓ #3 Cascara songo + 3:2 rhumba

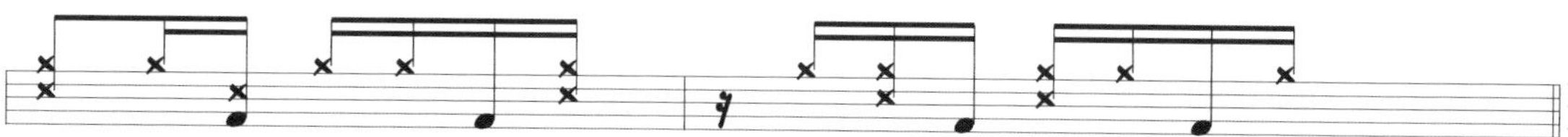

↓ dispursed snare accents

Mozambique with Tumbao

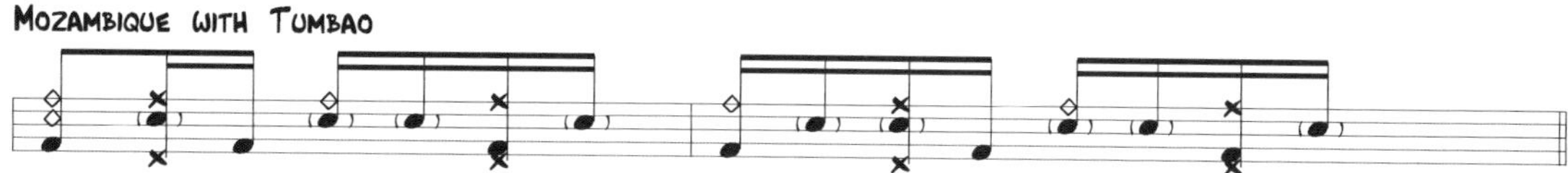

↓ Ride = Cascara #2

Dispersed Mozambique

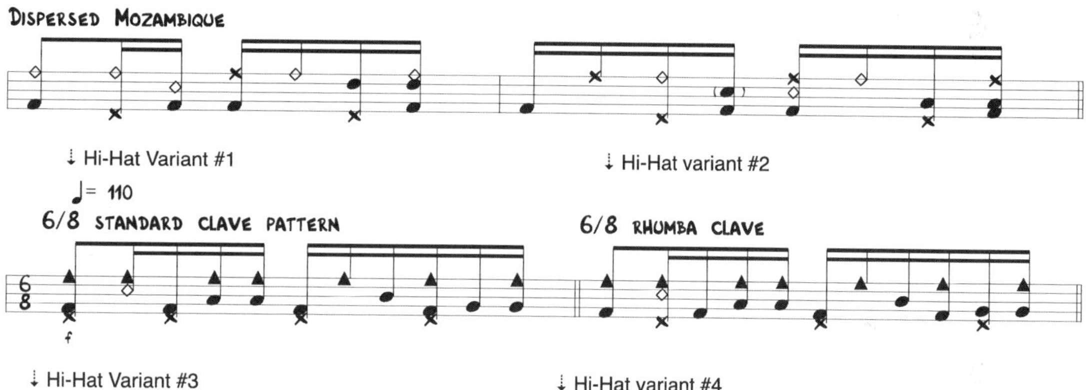

↓ Hi-Hat Variant #3

6/8 Son Clave

↓ Hi-Hat variant #4

6/8 Alternative

2/2

WARNING:

You are entering more sophisticated material

The remainder of this curriculum depends upon the student having **thoroughly studied** what has already been assigned up to this point. If you are not at a comfortable intermediate stage then I will go ahead and recommend that **you do not continue on**. Simply review all of the intermediate assignments. Give yourself some more time on it and then **return to this section and continue** with this curriculum. Otherwise, you will become frustrated and feel unaccomplished, bored, perhaps disheartened and feel as though things are not moving quickly enough. If you want to test yourself, go ahead and try the first page. If it is taking you too long, you'll need to review prior intermediate material. Avoid doing a "sneak peek" and trying to learn little bits here and there. That may provide temporary satisfaction, but it will not build your skills properly.

The assignments henceforth will therefore be a little more intense and a lot more demanding of your time. And if you have not absolutely conquered the fundamentals then this will be a bit overwhelming. But this is the reality of preparation. *Always be over-prepared!*

5.3 - Latin Rhythms – Level 2

Page Instructions

For the same reason you studied a lot of Jazz and Funk in this curriculum, you are about to continue your laborious journey in Latin percussion. You will gain a great deal of coordination and knowledge in the coming weeks. Study hard and be excited about the drummer you are about to become!

These are written in suggested tempos. You do **not** need to play them at the recommended speed. Just be able to play it confidently at whatever speed you can handle. The curriculum is divided so that you may comfortably manage your studies each week. If you are fortunate and have both the time and inclination to move beyond the recommended pace, congratulations! You're one of the few, and a rare breed! However, don't expect yourself to memorize all this material in any case. Just use it to build your coordination and move on, taking a few rhythms with you as you go.

Weekly Assignment week #1

- Rudiment: Single & Double Drag Tap – (figures 46 & 47) The **single and double** "drag tap" rudiments, by now should be simple to play. The most common problem with learning the names of rudiments is lack of application. It is not necessary to practice these all week. You should *learn* them, however. Please take the time to memorize them by name. The accents are important to focus on. The "drag" is represented by a set of grace notes before the beat. Remember that these grace notes are delivered *before* the count. That is, before the beat of "1." They are called "drags" because they are delivered before the beat and are not verbally counted. You will see the sticking written both directions for the *single drag tap*. That is so you know how to perform it both ways.
- **Rhythms**: *6/8 Rhumba clave over Samba* – This could take all week to master. Learn it "one beat at a time."

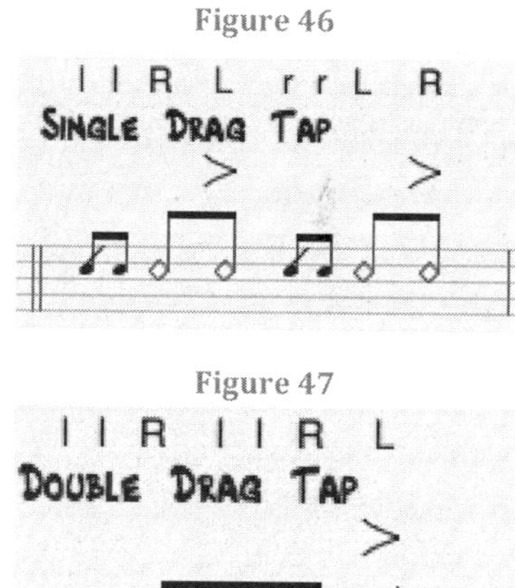

Weekly Assignment week #2

- **Rhythms**: *Gahu* – Your first introduction to true African rhythms. Notice the hi-hat foot and the cross-stick. You may use any toms you wish to. But there is *no snare* in it.
- **Rhythms**: *Tumbao with Cascara* – The LH is going to begin on the first note as a rimshot. You will repeat this rhythm. When you are comfortable, move the rimshot to the second snare note ('&'); then move it to the third note, then the fourth and so on, until you have completed accenting all the snare notes. *Permutation*, in this sense, is "changing the lineal order of a set of objects."

Weekly Assignment week #3

- **Rhythms**: *Mozambique Songo variation* – based on a variant of "Spain" by Chick Corea, performed by Dave Weckl.
- **Rhythms**: *Guaguanco* (wh'-whan-ko) – is a type of Cuban rhumba. This particular guaguanco is a 3:2 pattern on the ride cymbal. You will perform with the hi-hat on **upbeat** and on the **downbeat**.
- **Rhythms**: *Advanced Guaguanco* – Cowbell and cross-sticking and extra toms added. If you can't do this one right now, that is okay. It is indeed a challenge. I placed the sticking above the exercise in 'RH, LH, Both' sequence for you to make it easier.

Weekly Assignment week #4

- **Rhythms:** *Bossa* – All four bossa rhythms. Note: There is only one RH ride cymbal pattern. The others are RH hi-hat.
- **Rhythms:** *Samba (variation with toms)* – RH ride cymbal pattern.
- **Rhythms:** *Songo #1* – Basic songo. Think of it as a linear groove
- **Rhythms:** *Songo #2* – Same as previous rhythm, with a bossa hi-hat pattern.

Weekly Assignment week #5

- **Rhythms**: *Mozambique Songo with 2/3 Rhumba* – Notice the accents. I would advice learning this using the *layering* method.
- **Rhythms**: *Mozambique Songo with bell and HH* – Same thing as previous exercise. Add hi-hat foot and the ride cymbal with accents on the bell.
- **Rhythms**: *Mozambique Samba* – This is a linear rhythm over a samba kick pattern.

Weekly Assignment week #6

- **Rhythms**: *Mozambique Tumbao* – Hands: Ride cymbal with bell accents; x-stick. Feet: Hi-hat on upbeat; tumbao kick drum. Method to learn this rhythm: 1) feet, 2) hands, then 3) altogether.
- **Rhythms**: *Mozambique Samba (with dispersed cowbell)* – This is your first introduction to dispersing your hands to various *voices* on the drumkit. To *disperse* means to, "spread or distribute from a fixed or constant source." That means, move your hands around to other voices; be creative! Don't worry so much about the left hand. If you feel you can move it around as written it will only help you. But the point of this exercise is to be more creative with the right hand so that you are not so stationary or static sounding.
- **Rhythms**: *Songo - Basic 1/4 Ride with HH foot* – Just a refresher, adding a little more to it. You should be able to do this already.

Weekly Assignment week #7

- **Rhythms**: *Basic Cascara pattern* – Amazing what you can do with a basic 16th note linear groove when you add accents/rimshots to it. That is all this is. But get used to the feel. This is a good one to have in your war chest.
- **Rhythms**: *Cascara, Songo* – Notice the bell of the ride has been replaced with an actual cowbell. This is a real-life application of this rhythm. If you can play this smoothly, you'll be way ahead of your competition.
- **Rhythms**: *Cascara, Songo* and *Toms* – Same rhythm, LH dispersed around the kit.
- **Rhythms:** *Cascara variation* – where it says, "Look!" is where the variant is. This is my preferred cascara. I hope you were observing the hi-hat foot through these!

5.3 - Latin Rhythms

Level 2

5.3 - Latin Rhythms

2/2

5.3 - Latin Rhythms

Level 2

5.3 - Latin Rhythms

2/4

5.3 - Latin Rhythms

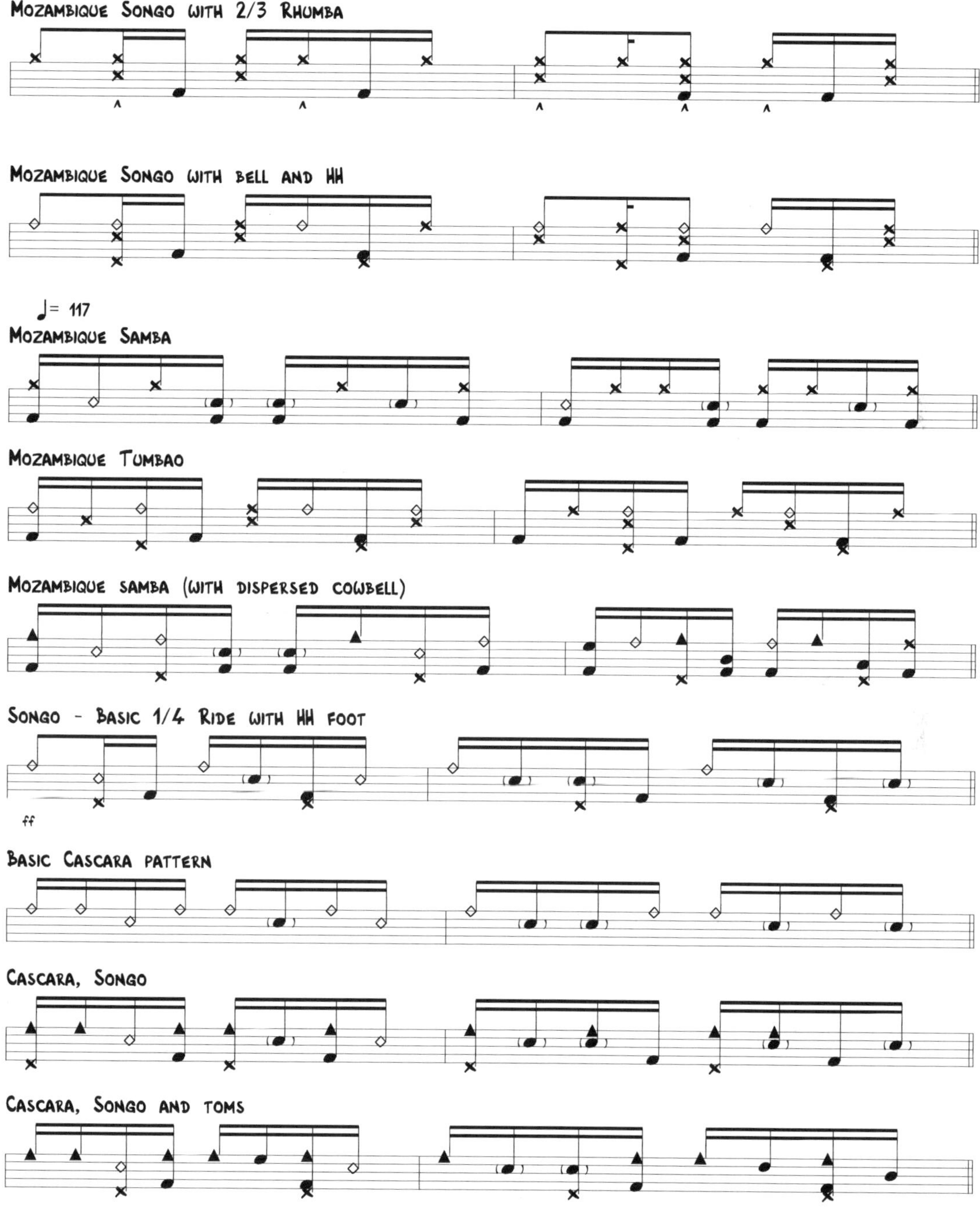

5.3 - Latin Rhythms

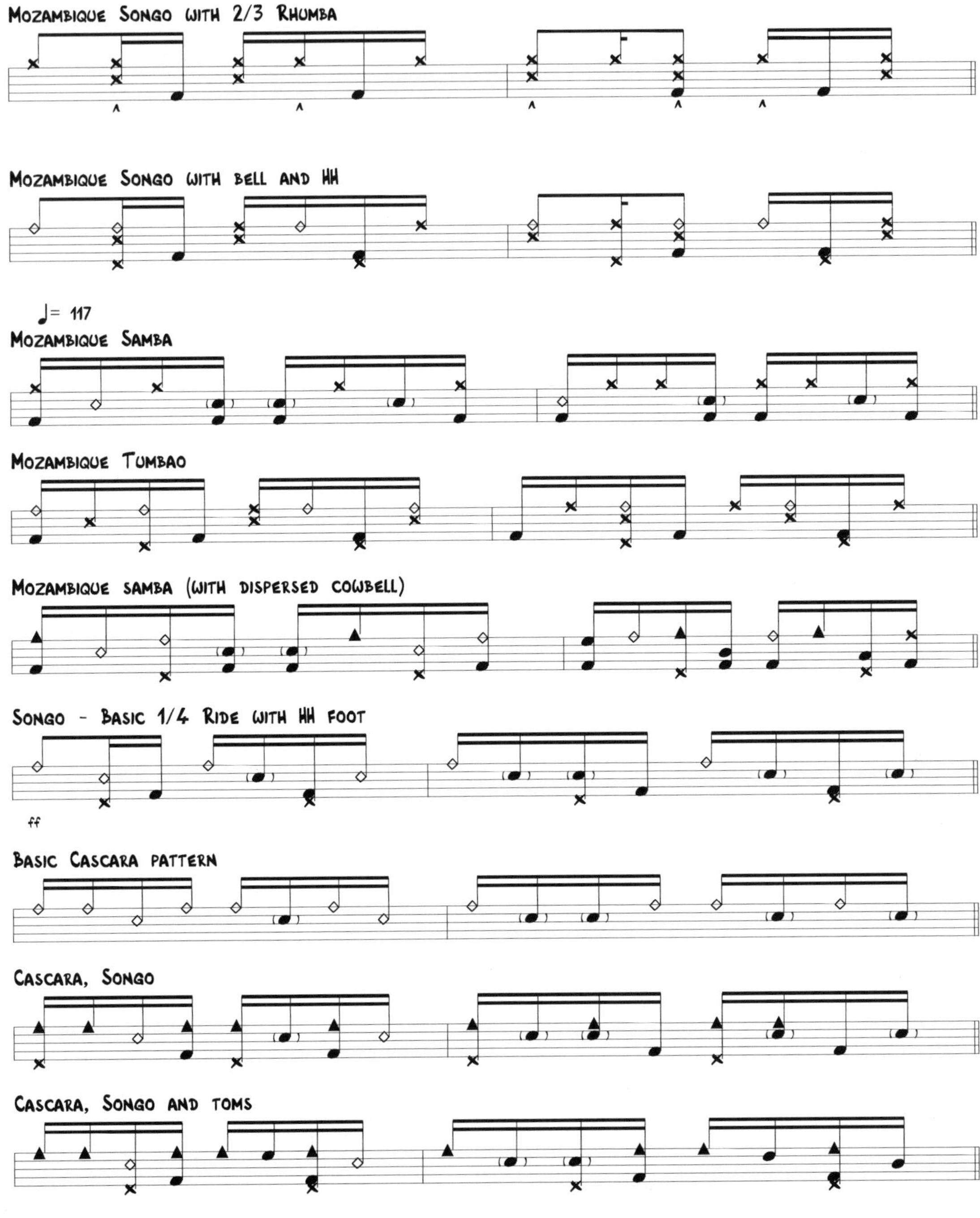

3/4

5.3 - Latin Rhythms

Cascara Variation

4/4

5.4 - Latin Rhythms – Level 3

Page Instructions

Welcome to level three. I wanted to call this the *Advanced* Latin Rhythms. However, that was misleading.

Whenever you see 'Adv' in front of something, unless you are bold, you may avoid it. For instance, I'm not going to actually assign you the "*Adv Combo: Rhumba 3-2 (LF), tumbao (RF), cascara (RH), 2-3 Rhumba (LH)*" because it's quite difficult. It is there, however to demonstrate how you can infinitely combine any set of four ostinatos to create a fantastic and impressive rhythm. Yes, I can play that one. It took nearly a week to get it comfortably. The notes say, "Cowbell and HH foot are same voice" meaning that the LF is played on a *Gijate* device attached to a block or cowbell.

Weekly Assignment week #1

- Rudiment: Single Dragadiddle – (figure 48) This rudiment is based upon a single paradiddle, which means there can be a double-dragadiddle based upon a double-paradiddle. The first 'rr' is officially a *drag* but technically it's just two 32nd notes since the 'drag' does not precede the first note. You should already know to *bounce* all doubles and drags. The accent means that the 'drag' is louder than the rest of the sticking.

Figure 48

- **Rhythms**: *Samba over Mozambique* – Pushing the envelope a bit further, another variant of samba + Mozambique. Always push yourself further. Experiment and try new things.
- **Song:** *Roll the Bones* (Rush) - Last song of the curriculum. I have created a very detailed note-for-note-chart. This song incorporates almost everything you have learned so far into one song. **You will be on your own as to how fast you learn it** based upon how much time you have and how much you can absorb.

  - Pay special attention to the quads and fast triplets over snare and toms. The kick drum rhythm is particularly important. If the kick drum part does not match up with the bass guitar, it will simply not sound good at all.
  - There is one measure where a 64th kick is used on page two, second measure of the instrumental. Watch out for getting the Bridge section correct. If you are lucky, you will possess an electronic kit; if you are super lucky it will have the exact drum sounds needed for this. But it doesn't matter truly. Just use your drums to the best of your ability to emulate it.
  - Watch for the Outro – There is a quads fill. Following that, the first note is Snare+Crash, not Kick+Crash.
  - The song fades out. Just end it where you wish.
  - **Strive to learn a page every week.**

Send me a video of you playing this song! I want to see it. I promise *I won't critique it unless you ask me to.*

Weekly Assignment week #2

- **Rhythms**: *Samba (Busy LH)* – a very useful rhythm. Once you get it you have the coordination to modify it various different ways, and various time signatures.

Weekly Assignment week #3

- **Rhythms**: *Tumbao #1* – Still using the Mozambique on RH
- **Rhythms**: *Tumbao #2* – Look carefully at the RH ostinato. It has changed to "1e-a, 2-&-, 3-&a, -e-a" rhythm.
- **Rhythms**: *Tumbao #3* – Again, the RH ostinato has changed. The bell accents are not as important. You can use a cowbell also.

Weekly Assignment week #4

- **Rhythms**: *Songo with "-&a#" Ride* – Learn this one layer at a time. Start with the songo ostinato, and then add the RH, then the LF. Go back and learn RH + LF very slowly. By the time this is natural (20 minutes?) you should be able to throw it all together.
- **Rhythms**: *Songo ¼ bell, toms, HH* – Another very valuable skill.

In all we, as instructor and student, have covered a giant range of skills and coordination using this material. But by no means has it covered everything possible. If you wish to go over the advance rhythms now, you may do so. It is not necessary, but it is advisable to return to the beginning of this book and tighten up what you can, absorb whatever you already have not, and perhaps move to the intermediate or the advanced concepts that may be on each page.

I hope to see you again in the next curriculum, and I hope you have become the drummer you wanted to be. Please keep me informed of your progress. As an instructor, I do very much care to know just how far you have gone, what you have achieved, your ideas (even strange ones) on drumming and what inspires you most.

Thank you for putting your confidence in me as an instructor. Please know that regardless of how where we began, or how far we will continue as instructor and student, I have enjoyed every minute of it. Because I enjoy teaching, and I enjoy seeing students grow.

Tyrone Steele
http://tyronesteele.com

5.4 - Latin Rhythms

Level 3

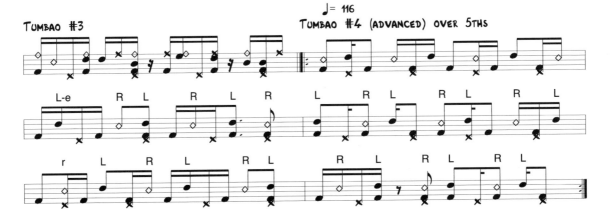

5.4 - Latin Rhythms

5.4 - Latin Rhythms

Level 3

5.4 - Latin Rhythms

2/2

Student Notes

Page/Chapter/Section	Technique/Concept	Notes/Comments

Addendum: Top Drummers of the Day

Artist	Born	Died	Age	Performed with:	And with:	And with:	And ...	And ...	And ...
Alan White	1949		66	Yes (2)	John Lennon				
Alex Van Halen	1953		62	Van Halen					
Art Blakey	1919	1990	71	Hank Mobley	The Messengers				
Benny Greb	1980		35						
Bernard Purdie	1939		76	Aretha Franklin	Roberta Flack	Miles Davis			
Billy Higgins	1936	2001	65	Thelonious Monk	Pat Metheny				
Bill Bruford	1949		66	Yes (1)	Frank Zappa	King Crimson			
Billy Cobham	1944		71	Miles Davis	George Duke				
Buddy Rich	1917	1987	70	Self					
Butch Miles	1944		71	Count Basie					
Carmine Appice	1946		69	Vanilla Fudge	Rod Stewart	Paul Stanley			
Carter Beauford	1957		58	Dave Matthews					
Chad Smith	1961		54	Red Hot Chili Peppers					
Chris Coleman	1979		36	New Kids on the Block	Chaka Khan	Israel and New Breed			
Danny Carey	1961		54	Tool	Green Jelly				
Dave Weckl	1960		55	Chick Corea	Michael Camillo	Simon& Garfunkel			
David Garibaldi	1946		69	Tower of Power					
Dennis Chambers	1959		56	Steely Dan	Carlos Santana	John Scofield			
Doane Perry	1954		61	Jethro Tull					
Dom Famularo	1953		62	Various					
Ed Blackwell	1929	1992	63	Ellis Marsalis	Ray Charles				
Elvin Jones	1927	2004	77	John Coltrane					
Freddie Gruber	1927	2011	84	Charlie Parker					
Gary Novak	1969		46	Chick Corea	Alanis Morissette	Lee Ritenour	George Benson		
Gavin Harrison	1963		52	porcupine tree					
Gene Krupa	1909	1973	64	Benny Goodman					
Ginger Baker	1939		76	Cream					
Gregg Bissonette	1959		56	Joe Satriani	David Lee Roth	Steve Vai	Carlos Santana		
Horacio Hernandez	1963		52	Michel Camilo	Carlos Santana				
Jack DeJohnette	1942		73	Miles Davis	Pat Metheny	Keith Jarrett			
Jeff Porcarro (son of Joe)	1954	1992	38	Toto (1)	Eric Clapton	Steely Dan	Dire Straits	Michael Jackson	Boz Scagggs
Jeff Sipe	1959		56	Bela Fleck	Jimmy Herring	Phish			
Jim Chapin	1919	2009	90	Tommy Dorsey	Casa Loma Orchestra				
Joe Morello	1928	2011	83	Dave Brubeck	Dave Brubeck				
Joe Porcaro (father of jeff)	1930		85	Frank Sinatra	Pink Floyd	Natilie Cole	Monkey's	Madonna	
John Blackwell	1973		42	Prince	J.J. Jackson	Justin Timberlake			
John Bonham	1948	1980	32	Led Zeppelin					
John Panozzo	1948	1996	48	Styx (1)					
Jo (papa) Jones	1911	1985	74	Count Basie					
Joe (philly) Jones	1923	1985	62	Miles Davis					
JoJo Mayer	1963		52	Pohibited Beatz	Screaming Headless Torsos	Nerve			
Keith Carlock	1971		44	Steely Dan	Sting	John Mayer			
Keith Moon	1946	1978	32	The Who					
Kenny Clark	1914	1985	71	Dizzy Gillespie	Theolonious Monk	Charlie Parker			
Lee Pearson				Spyro Gyra	Mike Stern				
Louis Bellson	1924	2009	85	Benny Goodman	Tommy Dorsey	Duke Ellington			
Marco Minnemann	1970		45	Aristrocrats	Necrophagist				
Max Roach	1924	2007	83	Dizzy Gillespie	Theolonious Monk	Charlie Parker	Bud Powell	Clifford Brown	
Mike Mangini	1963		52	Dream Theater	Extreme	Steve Vai			
Mike Portnoy	1967		48	Dream Theater	Transatlantic	Sevenfold	Winery Dogs		
Mitch Mitchell	1947	2008	61	Jimmy Hendrix					
Neil Peart	1952		63	Rush					
Pat Petrillo	1964		51	Gloria Gaynor	Patti LaBelle				
Peter Erskine	1954		61	Elvis Costello	Joni Mitchell				
Phil Collins	1951		64	Genesis	Eric Clapton	Tears for Fears	Peter Gabriel	Robert Plant	Band-Aid
Rick Latham	1955		60	Edgar Winter Group					
Ringo Starr	1940		75	The Beatles					
Rod Morgenstein	1953		62	Winger	Dixie Dregs				
Roy Haynes	1925		90						
Sanford Moeller	1886	1960	74	George M. Cohen	Vaudville				
Simon Phillips	1957		58	Toto (2)	Tears for Fears	Jeff Beck	Pete Townsend		
Steve Gadd	1945		70	Paul Simon	Steely Dan	Chick Corea	McCartney	Frank Sinatra	Eric Clapton
Steve Jordan	1957		58	Eric Clapton	Boz Scaggs	John Mayer	Bruno Mars	LeAnn Rimes	Bruce Springsteen
Steve Smith	1954		61	Journey					
Stewart Copeland	1952		63	Police					
Terry Bozzio	1950		65	Frank Zappa	Jeff Beck				
Tom Knight	1968		47	TLC	Adam Nitti	AIM			
Thomas Lang	1967		48	Var. European rock					
Todd Sucherman	1969		46	Styx (2)					
Tony Royster Jr	1984		31	Jay-Z					
Tony Williams	1945	1997	52	Miles Davis					
Vinnie Colaiuta	1956		59	Chick Corea	Frank Zappa	Herbie Hancock	Jeff Beck	Sting	
Virgil Donati	1958		57	Planet X	Steve Vai				

Curriculum Outline

Section I. Introduction Material

a) Design, Purpose and Intent
b) Technique, Stick Grip and Pedal Control
c) Foot Position Diagrams
d) Hi-Hat Pedal Techniques
e) Steps to Learning Any Rhythm
f) Tips for Parents
g) The First Drumset
h) Student Assignment Sheet
i) How To Read Dotted Notes
j) The Proper Care and Feeding of Your Drumkit
k) Drumkit Ergonomics – Setting up

Section II. Reference Materials

a) Reading Music
b) Triplet Combination Patterns
c) Rudiments (PAS adopted)

Section III. Warm-up and Exercises

a) Mirroring the hands
b) Forearm Slap
c) Wrist Trapping
d) Leg Pressure
e) Bouncing Stick Drop
f) Open-close Palm Coordination
g) Foot heel-toe tapping

Section IV. Curriculum

Level One: **Beginner (no belt)** Basics

1.1 - All 8th and 16th Note Rhythms
1.2 - All 8th Note Triplet Beats
1.3 - All 8th Note Triplet Rhythms
- Rudiment: The Single-Stroke Roll

1.4 - All Shuffle Rhythms
1.5 - All 16th Note Beats
- Rudiment: The Double-Stroke Roll

Level Two: **Beginner concepts (white belt)** – Grooves and Exercises

2.1 - Swing Basics
- Rudiment: The Flam

2.2 - 6/8 Exercises
- Rudiment: The Single-Stroke Triplet
- Song: *Blue Jeans Blues* (ZZ Top) – **OR** –
- Song: *Wagon Wheel* (Old Crow Medicine)

2.3 - Rock and Funk Beats

- Rudiment: Drag Triplet
- Song: *Sweet Home Alabama* (Lynard Skynard)

2.4 - Alternating 16ths and Alternate Sticking
- Rudiment: Understanding Stoke Rolls – 5,7,9,10
- Rudiment: The Drag
- Rudiment: Flam Drag
- Song: *Wonderful Tonight* (Eric Clapton) – **OR** –
- Song: *Legs* (ZZ Top)

2.5 - Open Hi-Hat Reading Exercises
- Rudiment: The Swiss-Six & the 6-Stroke Roll
- Song: *Smoke On Water* (Deep Purple)

2.6 - Triplet rhythm Reading Exercise
- Song: *The Sky is Crying* (Stevie Ray Vaughn)

2.7 - Kick Drum Reading Exercise #1 (8th notes)
- Song: *Pour Some Sugar On Me* (Def Leppard)

2.8 - Beginner Snare Solos

Level Three: **Higher Beginner (yellow belt)** – Fills, Swing and Funk

3.1 - Paradiddle Fills
- Rudiment: The Single Paradiddles
- Rudiment: The Double Paradiddles
- Song: *Nothing Else Matters* (Metallica)

3.2 - Paradiddle Fills – Advanced (no instructions)

3.3 - Inverted Paradiddle Grooves
- Song: *Fire* (Jimmy Hendrix) – just the first verse/chorus

3.4 - Swing Exercises

3.5 - Hi-Hat Up-Beat Exercises
- Song: *American Idiot* (Green Day)

3.6 - Funk Exercises

3.7 - Funk Grooves
- Song: *Play That Funky Music Whiteboy (Wildcherry)*

Level Four: **Intermediate (orange belt)** – Getting More Complex

4.1 - Dotted Eights
- Song: *Bring Me To Life (Evanescence)*

4.2 - Odd Meter Rhythms
- Rudiment: Flam Accent & Swiss Army Triplet

4.3 - Odd Meter Exercises
- Song: *Schism (Tool) – beginning instrumental & verse*

4.4 - Linear Exercises
- Rudiment: Flam Tap and Inverted Flam Tap

4.5 - Triples, Quads, Quints
- Song: *La Grange* (ZZ Top)

4.6 - (a) Music Styles 1
(b) Music Styles 2 - Latin

4.7 - Kick Drum Reading Exercise #2 (16th Notes)

Level Five: **Higher Intermediate (green belt)** – expanding your drumming

5.1 - Linear Fills and Rhythms
- Song: *Losing It (Rush)*
- Rudiment: Buzz Roll

5.2 - Latin Rhythms – Level 1

5.3 - Latin Rhythms – Level 2
- Rudiment: Single & Double Drag Tap

5.4 - Latin Rhythms – Level 3
- Song: *Roll The Bones (Rush)*
- Rudiment: Single Dragadiddle

Index

About The Author

Tyrone Steele is a freelance drummer based in the Atlanta area. He proudly endorses *Bootleg Drum Company* and *Soultone* Cymbals. Tyrone maintains memberships with BMI and Atlanta chapter of the Grammy Recording Academy.

He has twice opened for Joe Diffie and performs as an independent drummer. Tyrone is often a guest instructor at the Atlanta Institute of Music and Media, and teaches from his home studio as well as at various music stores around the northern Atlanta, GA area. He is trained in fusion, Latin, be-bop, rock, and metal. Tyrone is a staple in the drumming community and comes highly recommended by many artists, instructors and peers for his attention to detail, timeliness, meter, creativity and ability to drive any band or music style. Tyrone is a multi-instrumental composer and lyricist.

His name has appeared in the Georgia Country music awards:

"*Tyrone is the consummate perfectionist and his drums have a tone that is remarkable and I think that is just one of many things that sets him apart. He is easily the best drummer I have ever played with.*"

— JC Bridwell, November 2013

Tyrone began drumming in 1983. He served in the Marine Corps from 1989-1995. In 2011, upon completing a Master of Divinity and M.A.R. program at Liberty Theological Seminary, he began his musical education at the Atlanta Institute of Music, and consistently received the Merit Scholarship for outstanding performance. He was trained by Tom Knight and Creig Harber, and personally instructed by Dave Weckl.

His main drumming influences are: *Tom Knight, Benny Greb, Carter Beauford, Chris Coleman, Dave Weckl, Gary Novak, John Blackwell, Heracio Hernandez, Lee Pearson, David Garibaldi, Marco Minnemann, JoJo Mayer, Steve Gadd, Steve Smith, Vinnie Colaiuta, John Bonham, Neil Peart.*

You can find his studio videos, performance information and schedule: **http://tyronesteele.com**
Tyrone is open to contact for any questions at:
tyrone@tyronesteele.com

Made in the USA
San Bernardino, CA
21 April 2015